Pro REST API Development with Node.js

Fernando Doglio

Apress®

Pro REST API Development with Node.js

Fernando Doglio
La Paz, Canelones
Uruguay

ISBN-13 (pbk): 978-1-4842-0918-9 ISBN-13 (electronic): 978-1-4842-0917-2
DOI 10.1007/978-1-4842-0917-2

Library of Congress Control Number: 2015941272

Distributed to the book trade worldwide by Springer Science+Business Media New York, 233 Spring Street, 6th Floor, New York, NY 10013. Phone 1-800-SPRINGER, fax (201) 348-4505, e-mail `orders-ny@springer-sbm.com`, or visit `www.springeronline.com`. Apress Media, LLC is a California LLC and the sole member (owner) is Springer Science + Business Media Finance Inc (SSBM Finance Inc). SSBM Finance Inc is a Delaware corporation.

For information on translations, please e-mail `rights@apress.com`, or visit `www.apress.com`.

Apress and friends of ED books may be purchased in bulk for academic, corporate, or promotional use. eBook versions and licenses are also available for most titles. For more information, reference our Special Bulk Sales–eBook Licensing web page at `www.apress.com/bulk-sales`.

Any source code or other supplementary material referenced by the author in this text is available to readers at `www.apress.com`. For detailed information about how to locate your book's source code, go to `www.apress.com/source-code/`.

Printed on acid-free paper

To my loving wife, without whom this book would've never happened...

Thank you!

Contents at a Glance

Contents

About the Author

Fernando Doglio has worked as a web developer for the past 10 years. In that time, he has come to love the Web, and has had the opportunity to work with most leading technologies, such as PHP, Ruby on Rails, MySQL, Node. js, Angular.js, AJAX, REST APIs, and others.

In his spare time, Fernando likes to tinker and learn new things, which is why his GitHub account keeps getting new repos every month. He's also a big open source supporter, trying to bring new people to it with the help of the site he created at `lookingforpullrequests.com`. When not programming, he is spending time with his family.

Fernando can be contacted on Twitter `@deleteman123`.

About the Technical Reviewer

Jose Dieguez Castro is a senior system administrator currently employed as a freelance consultant. He has worked on a wide range of projects—from small to large infrastructures, in private to public sectors. When is asked about his specialty, he replies, "Get the job done."

Jose also thinks of himself as a developer who cares too much about software *libre*. Photography, sports, music, and reading are his ways to free his mind from work. He can be reached at `jose@jdcastro.eu`.

Acknowledgments

I'd like to thank the amazing technical reviewer involved in the project, Jose Dieguez Castro, whose great feedback was a crucial contribution to the making of this book.

I'd also like to thank the rest of the Apress editorial team, whose guidance helped me through the process of writing this, my first book.

Introduction

These days, everyone is finding a new way to interconnect systems; the Internet of Things (IoT), for instance, is the new kid on the block, but who knows what will come later.

The point is that in order to interconnect systems, as an architect, you're better off using standard methods that allow for a faster adoption of your technology. In particular, APIs allow for the creation of standards and can work under known and well-tested core technologies like HTTP.

If you add to that a well-defined style guide like REST, you've got yourself the means to create a scalable, technology agnostic, and uniform interface for your services to be consumed by your clients.

Welcome to *Pro REST API Development with Node.js*. This book will cover REST, API development, and finally, how these two mix up with Node.js.

Starting from a theoretic point of view, you'll learn how REST came to be, who created it, and its characteristics. Later, you'll move toward the practical side by going over API development and the lessons that years of experience from the community have taught us. Finally, you'll move into a fully practical approach, and you'll see how Node.js and its modules can help create a RESTful API.

The final chapters will be 100% practical, going over a real-world example of a RESTful API developed in Node.js. I will cover everything from the requirement-gathering process, to tools selection, and through actual development, and finally, you'll land in troubleshooting-land, where I'll discuss the different things that can go wrong and how to tackle them.

Now sit back, relax, and enjoy the reading.

CHAPTER 1

REST 101

Nowadays, the acronym REST has become a buzzword, and as such, it's being thrown into the digital wind very carelessly by a lot of tech people without fully understanding what it really means. Just because you can interact with a system using HTTP, and send JSON back and forth, doesn't mean it's a RESTful system. REST is a lot more than that—and that is what we'll cover in this chapter.

Let's start where it all began, with Roy Fielding's paper, going over the main characteristics of his idea. I'll try to explain the main aspects of it, the constraints he added and why. I'll go over some examples and then jump backward, into the past, because even though REST has proven to be a huge jump forward regarding distributed systems interconnection, before Fielding's paper became popular, developers were still looking for solutions to the problem: how to easily interconnect a nonhomogeneous set of systems.

I'll do a quick review of the options developers had back then to interconnect systems, mainly going over SOAP and XML-RPC (the two main players before REST).

In the end, I'll jump back to our current time, comparing the advantages that REST brought us and thus showing why is it so popular today.

But first, a small clarification is in order: as you'll read in just a few minutes, REST is *protocol independent* (as long as the protocol has support for a URI scheme), but for the sake of this book and since we're focusing on API design, let's assume that the protocol we're using is HTTP, which will simplify explanations and examples. And as long as you keep in mind that the same is true for other protocols (like FTP), then you'll be fine.

Where Did It All Start?

This whole thing started with Roy Fielding, an American computer scientist born in 1965. He is one of the main authors of the HTTP protocol[1] (the protocol that the entire Web infrastructure is based on). He is also one of the co-authors of the Apache Web server[2] and he was the chair of the Apache Software Foundation[3] for the first three years of its existence.

So, as you can see, Fielding has made a lot of great contributions to the IT world, especially regarding the Internet, but I think that his doctoral thesis is the thing that received the most attention and made his name known among a lot of people who otherwise wouldn't have heard of him.

In the year 2000, Fielding presented his doctoral dissertation, *Architectural Styles and the Design of Network-based Software Architecture.*[4] In it he coined the term *REST*, an architectural style for distributed hypermedia systems.

Electronic supplementary material The online version of this chapter (doi:10.1007/978-1-4842-0917-2_1) contains supplementary material, which is available to authorized users.

[1]See `https://www.ietf.org/rfc/rfc2616.txt`.
[2]See `http://httpd.apache.org/`.
[3]See `http://www.apache.org/`.
[4]See `http://www.ics.uci.edu/~fielding/pubs/dissertation/rest_arch_style.htm`.

F. Doglio, *Pro REST API Development with Node.js*, DOI 10.1007/978-1-4842-0917-2_1

Put simply, REST (short for *REpresentational State Transfer*) is an architectural style defined to help create and organize distributed systems. The key word from that definition should be *style*, because an important aspect of REST (and which is one of the main reasons books like this one exist) is that it is an architectural style—not a guideline, not a standard, or anything that would imply that there are a set of hard rules to follow in order to end up having a RESTful architecture.

And because it is a style, and there is no Request for Comments (RFC) out there to define it, it's subject to misinterpretations from the people reading about it. Not only that, but some go as far as to leave parts out, and implement a subset of its features, which in turn leads to a widespread and incomplete REST ideal, leaving out features that would otherwise be useful and help your system's users.

The main idea behind REST is that a distributed system, organized RESTfully, will improve in the following areas:

- *Performance*: The communication style proposed by REST is meant to be efficient and simple, allowing a performance boost on systems that adopt it.
- *Scalability of component interaction*: Any distributed system should be able to handle this aspect well enough, and the simple interaction proposed by REST greatly allows for this.
- *Simplicity of interface*: A simple interface allows for simpler interactions between systems, which in turn can grant benefits like the ones previously mentioned.
- *Modifiability of components*: The distributed nature of the system, and the separation of concerns proposed by REST (more on this in a bit), allows for components to be modified independently of each other at a minimum cost and risk.
- *Portability*: REST is technology and language agnostic, meaning that it can be implemented and consumed by any type of technology (there are some constraints that I'll go over in a bit, but no specific technology is enforced).
- *Reliability*: The stateless constraint proposed by REST (more on this later) allows for the easier recovery of a system after failure.
- *Visibility*: Again, the stateless constraint proposed has the added benefit of improving visibility, because any monitoring system doesn't need to look further than a single request message to determine the full state of said request (this will become clear once I talk about the constraints in a bit).

From this list, some direct benefits can be extrapolated:

- A component-centric design allows you to make systems that are very fault tolerant. Having the failure of one component not affect the entire stability of the system is a great benefit for any system.
- Interconnecting components is quite easy, minimizing the risks when adding new features or scaling up or down.
- A system designed with REST in mind will be accessible to a wider audience, thanks to its portability (as described earlier).With a generic interface, the system can be used by a wider range of developers.

In order to achieve these properties and benefits, a set of constraints were added to REST to help define a uniform connector interface.

REST Constraints

According to Fielding, there are two ways to define a system. One is to start from a blank slate, an empty whiteboard, with no initial knowledge of the system being built or the use of familiar components until the needs are satisfied. A second approach is to start with the full set of needs for the system, and constraints are added to individual components until the forces that influence the system are able to interact in harmony with each other.

REST follows the second approach. In order to define a REST architecture, a null-state is initially defined—a system that has no constraints whatsoever and where component differentiation is nothing but a myth—and constraints are added one by one.

Client-Server

The first constraint to be added is one of the most common ones on network-based architectures: *client-server*. A server is in charge of handling a set of services, and it listens for requests regarding said services. The requests, in turn, are made via a connector by a client system needing one of those services (see Figure 1-1).

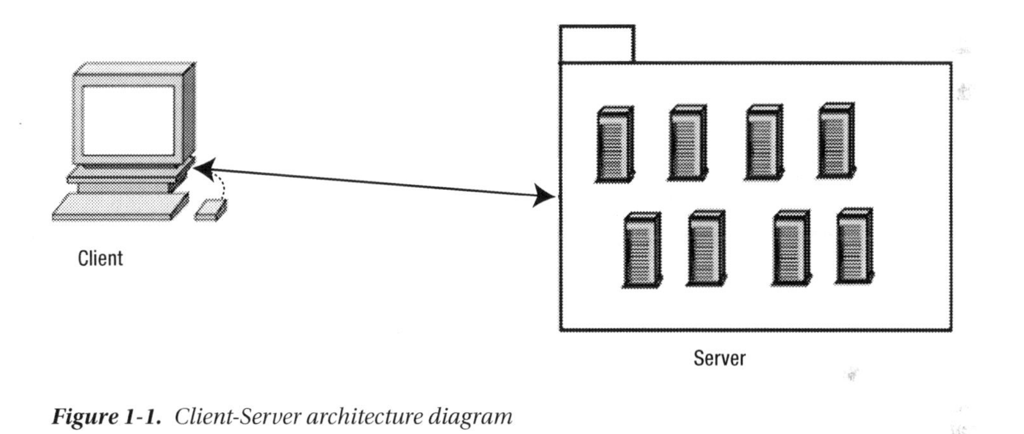

Figure 1-1. *Client-Server architecture diagram*

The main principle behind this constraint is the *separation of concerns*. It allows for the separation of front-end code (representation and possible UI-related processing of the information) from the server side code, which should take care of storage and server-side processing of the data.

This constraint allows for the independent evolution of both components, offering a great deal of flexibility by letting client applications improve without affecting the server code and vice-versa.

Stateless

The constraint to be added on top of the previous one is the *stateless* constraint (see Figure 1-2). Communication between client and server must be stateless, meaning that each request done from the client must have all the information required for the server to understand it, without taking advantage of any stored data.

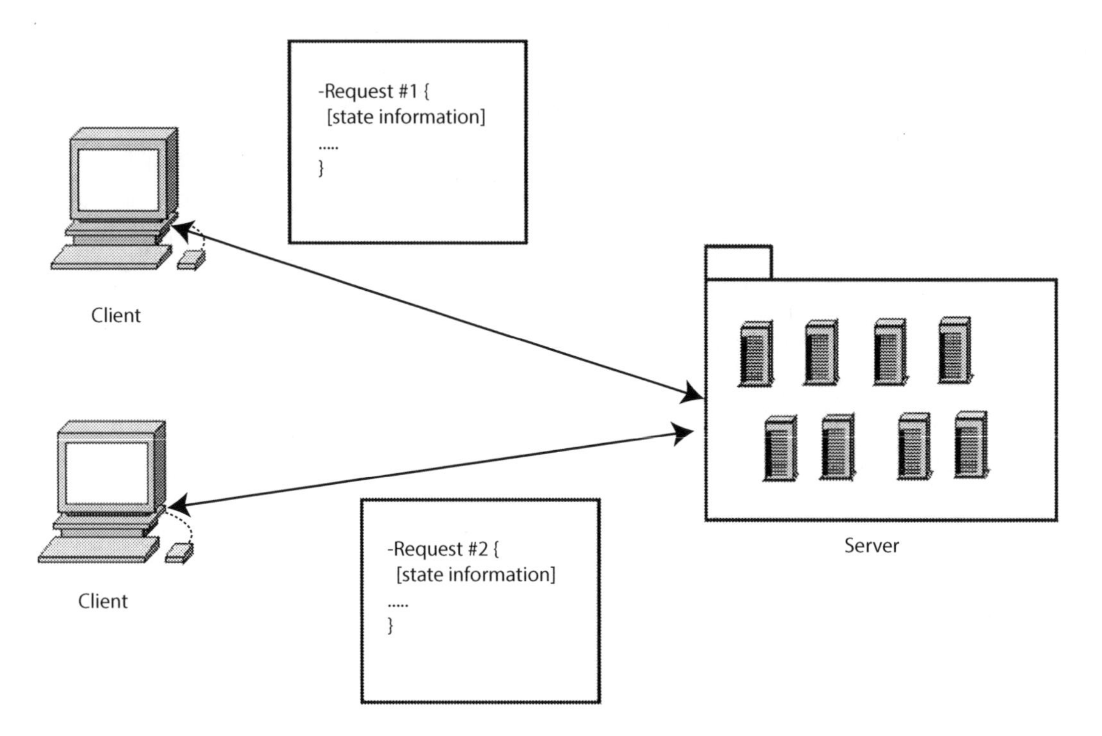

Figure 1-2. *Representation of the stateless constraint*

This constraint represents several improvements for the underlying architecture:

- *Visibility*: Monitoring the system becomes easy when all the information required is inside the request.
- *Scalability*: By not having to store data between requests, the server can free resources faster.
- *Reliability*: As mentioned earlier, a system that is stateless can recover from a failure much easier than one that isn't, since the only thing to recover is the application itself.
- *Easier implementation*: Writing code that doesn't have to manage stored state data across multiple servers is much easier to do, thus the full server-side system becomes simpler.

Although at first glance this constraint might seem nothing but good, as what normally happens, there is a trade-off. On one hand, benefits are gained by the system, but on the other side, network traffic could potentially be harmed by adding a minor overhead on every request from sending repeated state information. Depending on the type of system being implemented, and the amount of repeated information, this might not be an acceptable trade-off.

Cacheable

The *cacheable* constraint is added to the current set of constraints (see Figure 1-3). It proposes that every response to a request must be explicitly or implicitly set as cacheable (when applicable).

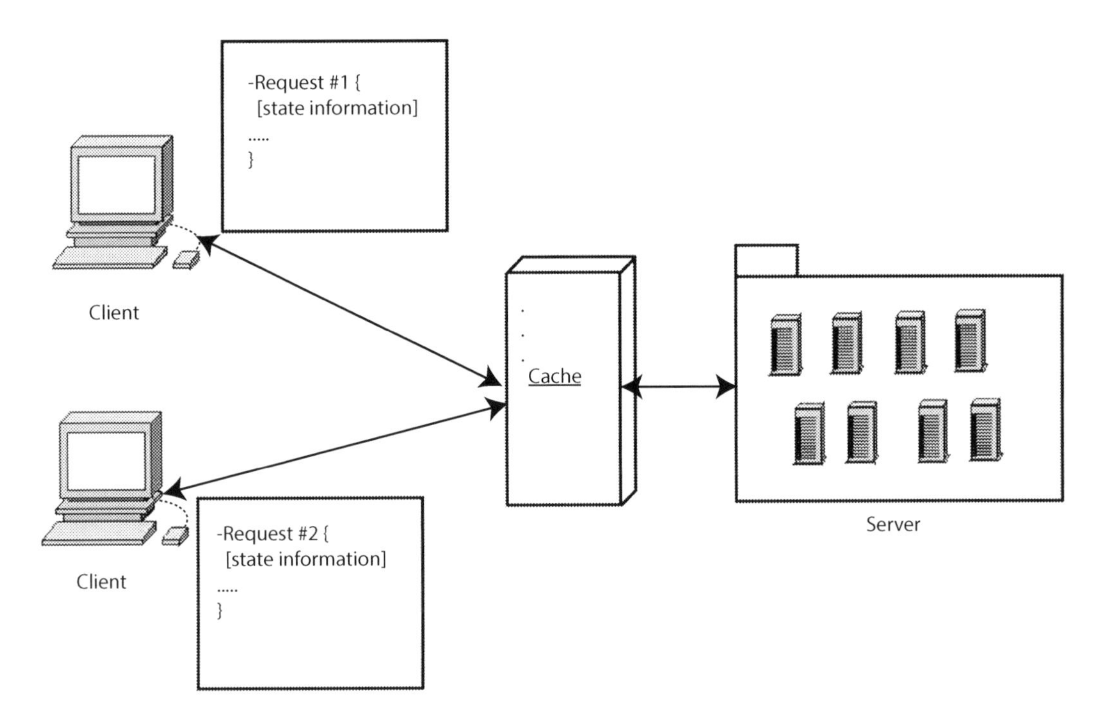

Figure 1-3. *Representation of a client-stateless-cache-server architecture*

By caching the responses, there are some obvious benefits that get added to the architecture: on the server side, some interactions (a database request, for example) are completely bypassed while the content is cached. On the client side, an apparent improvement of performance is perceived.

The trade-off with this constraint is the possibility of cached data being stale, due to poor caching rules. This constraint is, again, dependent on the type of system being implemented.

Note Figure 1-3 shows the cache as an external layer between the clients and the servers. This is only one possible implementation of it. The cache layer could be living inside the client (i.e., browser cache) or inside the servers themselves.

Uniform Interface

One of REST's main characteristics and winning points when compared to other alternatives is the *uniform interface* constraint. By keeping a uniform interface between components, you simplify the job of the client when it comes to interacting with your system (see Figure 1-4). Another major winning point here is that the client's implementation is independent of yours, so by defining a standard and uniform interface for all of your services, you effectively simplified the implementation of independent clients by giving them a clear set of rules to follow.

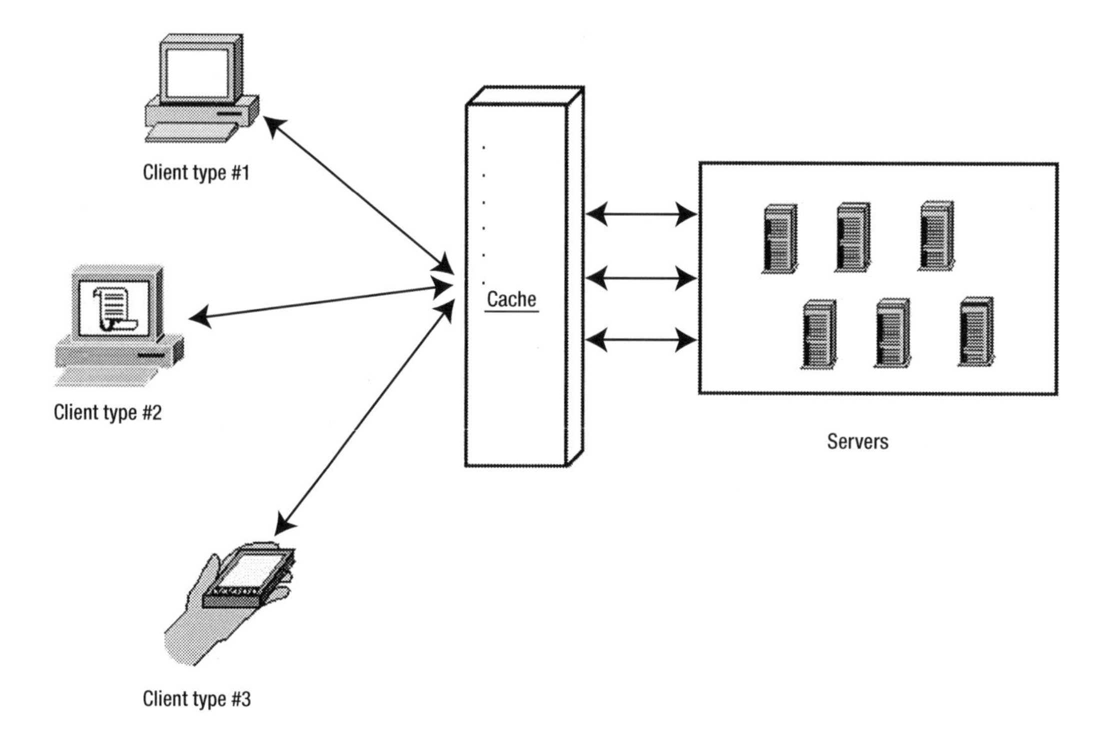

Figure 1-4. Different client types can interact seamlessly with servers thanks to the uniform interface

Said rules are not part of the REST style, but there are constraints that can be used to create such rules for each individual case.

This benefit doesn't come without a price, though; as with many other constraints, there is a trade-off here: having a standardized and uniform interface for all interactions with your system might harm performance when a more optimized form of communication exists. Particularly, the REST style is designed to be optimized for the Web, so the more you move away from that, the more inefficient the interface can be.

■ **Note** In order to achieve the uniform interface, a new set of constraints must be added to the interface: identification of resources, manipulation of resources through representation, self-descriptive messages, and hypermedia as the engine of application state (a.k.a HATEOAS). I'll discuss some of these constraints shortly.

Layered System

REST was designed with the Internet in mind, which means that an architecture that follows REST is expected to work properly with the massive amount of traffic that exists in the web of webs.

In order to achieve this, the concept of *layers* is introduced (see Figure 1-5). By separating components into layers, and allowing each layer to only use the one below and to communicate its output to the one above, you simplify the system's overall complexity and keep component coupling in check. This is a great benefit in all type of systems, especially when the complexity of such a system is ever-growing (e.g., systems with massive amounts of clients, systems that are currently evolving, etc.).

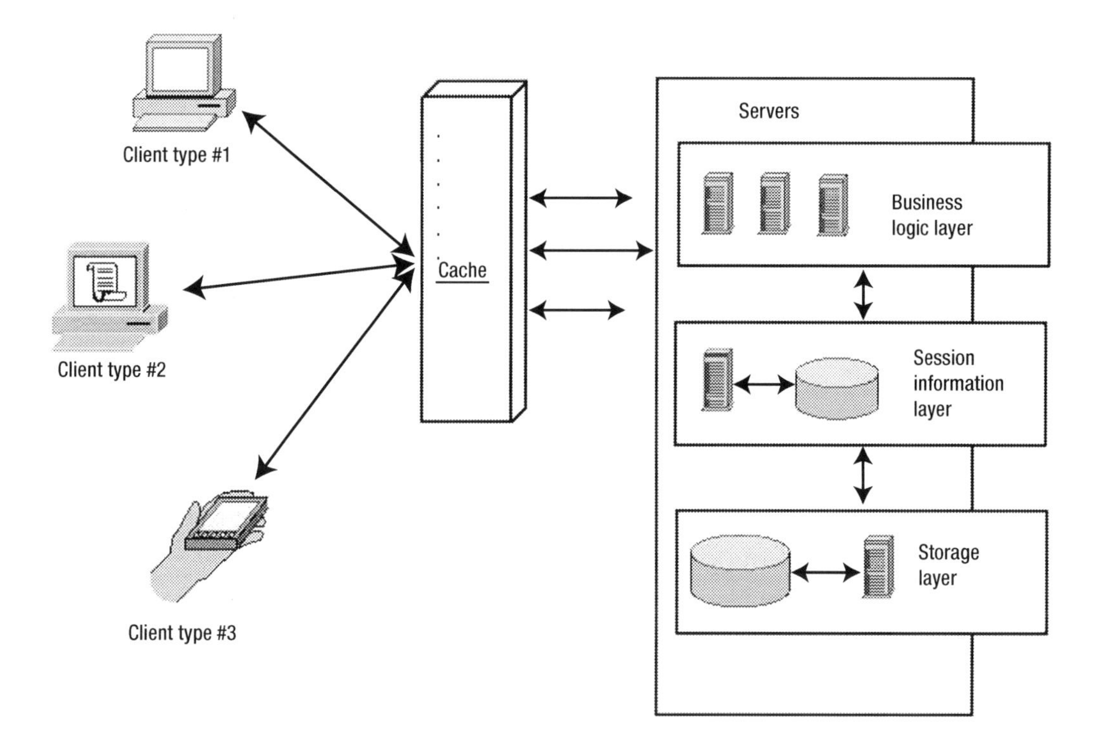

Figure 1-5. *Example of a multilayered architecture*

The main disadvantage of this constraint is that for small systems, it might add unwanted latency into the overall data flow, due to the different interactions between layers.

Code-on-Demand

Code-on-demand is the only optional constraint imposed by REST, which means that an architect using REST can choose whether or not to use this constraint, and either gains its advantages or suffers its disadvantages.

With this constraint, the client can download and execute code provided by the server (such as Java applets, JavaScript scripts, etc.). In the case of REST APIs (which is what this book focuses on), this constraint seems unnecessary, because the normal thing for an API client to do is just get information from an endpoint, and then process it however needed; but for other uses of REST, like web servers, a client (i.e., a browser) will probably benefit from this constraint (see Figure 1-6).

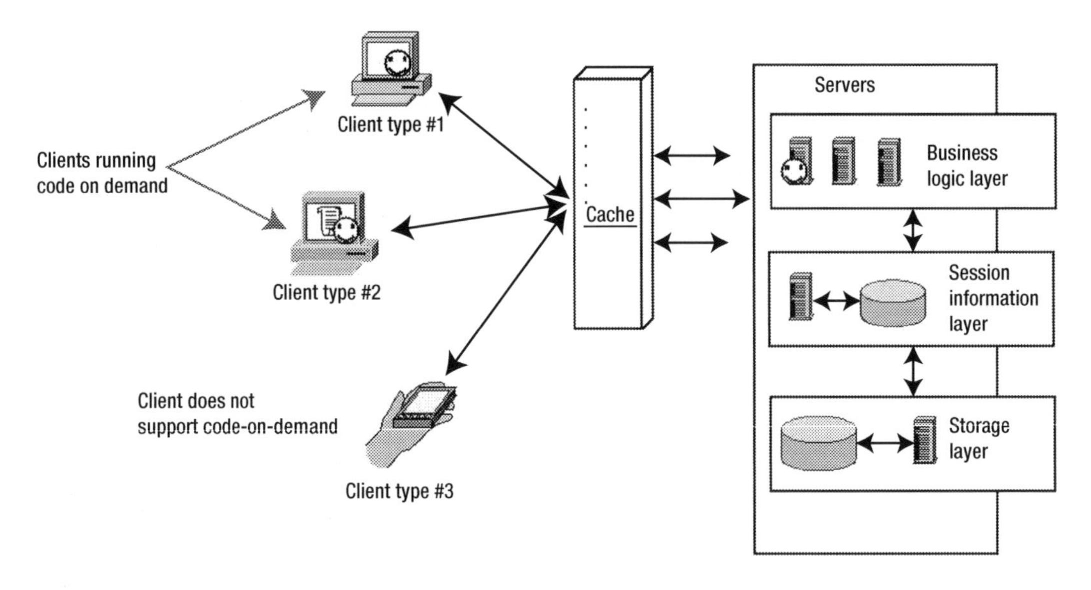

Figure 1-6. *How some clients might execute the code-on-demand, whereas others might not*

All of these constraints provide a set of virtual walls within which an architecture can move and still gain the benefits of the REST design style.

But let's take a step back. I initially defined REST as a design style for representational state transfer; in other words, you transfer the state of things by using *some kind* of representation. But what are these *"things"*? The main focus of a REST architecture is the resources, the owners of the state that you're transferring. Just like in a real state (almost), it's all about resources, resources, resources.

Resources, Resources, Resources

The main building blocks of a REST architecture are the *resources*. Anything that can be named can be a resource (a web page, an image, a person, a weather service report, etc.). Resources define what the services are going to be about, the type of information that is going to be transferred, and their related actions. The resource is the main entity from which everything else is born.

A resource is the abstraction of anything that can be conceptualized (from an image file, to a plain text document). The structure of a resource is shown in Table 1-1.

Table 1-1. *Resource Structure Description*

Property	Description
Representations	It can be any way of representing data (binary, JSON, XML, etc.). A single resource can have multiple representations.
Identifier	A URL that retrieves only one specific resource *at any given time.*
Metadata	Content-type, last-modified time, and so forth.
Control data	Is-modifiable-since, cache-control.

Representations

At its core, a *representation* is a set of bytes, and some metadata that describes these bytes. A single resource can have more than one representation; just think of a weather service report (which could act as a possible resource).

The weather report for a single day could potentially return the following information:

- The date the report is referencing
- The maximum temperature for the day
- The minimum temperature for the day
- The temperature unit to be used
- A humidity percentage
- A code indicating how cloudy the day will be (e.g., high, medium, low)

Now that the resource's structure is defined, here are a few possible representations of the same resource:

```
JSON
{
  "date": "2014-10-25",
  "max_temp": 25.5,
  "min_temp": 10.0,
  "temp_unit": "C",
  "humidity_percentage": 75.0,
  "cloud_coverage": "low"
}
```

```
XML
<?xml version='1.0' encoding='UTF-8' ?>
<root>
  <temp_unit value="C" />
  <humidity_percentage value="75.0" />
  <cloud_coverage value="low" />
  <date value="2014-10-25" />
  <min_temp value="10.0" />
  <max_temp value="25.5" />
</root>
```

Custom pipe-separated values:

```
2014-10-25|25.5|10.0|C|75.0|low
```

And there could be many more. They all successfully represent the resource correctly; it is up to the client to read and parse the information. Even when the resource has more than one representation, it is common for clients (due to simplicity of development) to only request one of them. Unless you're doing some sort of consistency check against the API, there is no point in requesting more than one representation of the same resource, is there?

There are two very popular ways to let the client request a specific representation on a resource that has more than one. The first one directly follows the principles described by REST (when using HTTP as a basis), called *content negotiation*, which is part of the HTTP standard. The second one is a simplified version of this, with limited benefits. For the sake of completeness, I'll quickly go over them both.

Content Negotiation

As mentioned, this methodology is part of the HTTP standard,[5] so it's the preferred way according to REST (at least when focused on API development on top of HTTP). It is also more flexible and provides further advantages than the other method.

It consists of the client sending a specific header with the information of the different content types (or types of representations) supported, with an optional indicator of how much supported/preferred that format is. Let's look at an example from the "Content Negotiation" page on Wikipedia:

```
Accept: text/html; q=1.0, text/*; q=0.8, image/gif; q=0.6, image/jpeg; q=0.6, image/*;
q=0.5, */*; q=0.1
```

This example is from a browser configured to accept various types of resources, but preferring HTML over plain text, and GIF or JPEG images over other types, but ultimately accepts any other content type as a last resort.

On the server side, the API is in charge of reading this header and finding the best representation for each resource, based on the client's preferences.

Using File Extensions

Even though this approach is not part of the REST proposed style, it is widely used and a fairly simple alternative to the somewhat more complex other option, so I'll cover it anyway.

During the last few years, using file extensions has become an alternative preferred over using content negotiation; it is a simpler version and it doesn't rely on a header being sent, but instead, it works with the concept of file extensions.

The extension portion of the file's name indicates the content type to the operating system and any other software trying to use it; so in the following case, the extension added to the resource's URL (unique identifier) indicates to the server the type of representation wanted.

```
GET /api/v1/books.json
GET /api/v1/books.xml
```

Both identifiers reference the same resource—the list of books, but they request a different representation of it.

■ **Note** This approach might seem easier to implement, and even understand, by humans, but it lacks the flexibility added by content negotiation, and should only be used if there is no real need for complex cases where multiple content types might be specified with their related preference.

Resource Identifier

The resource identifier should provide a unique way of identification at any given moment and it should provide the full path to the resource. A classic mistake is to assume it's the resource's ID on the storage medium used (i.e., the ID on the database). This means that you cannot consider a simple numeric ID as a resource identifier; you must provide the full path, and because we're basing REST on HTTP, the way to access the resource it to provide its full URI (*unique resource identifier*).

[5]See http://tools.ietf.org/html/rfc7231#section-5.3.

There is one more aspect to consider: the identifier of each resource must be able to reference it unequivocally at any given moment in time. This is an important distinction, because a URI like the following might reference *Harry Potter and the Half Blood Prince* for a certain period of time, and then *Harry Potter and the Deathly Hollows* one year later.:

```
GET /api/v1/books/last
```

This renders that URI as an invalid resource ID. Instead, each book needs a unique URI that is certain to not change over time; for example:

```
GET /api/v1/books/j-k-rowling/harry-potter-and-the-deathly-hollows
GET /api/v1/books/j-k-rowling/harry-potter-and-the-half-blood-prince
```

The identifiers are unique here, because you can safely assume that the author won't publish more books with the same title.

And to provide a valid example for getting the last book, you might consider doing something like this:

```
GET /api/v1/books?limit=1&sort=created_at
```

The preceding URI references the lists of books, and it asks for only one, sorted by its publish date, thus rendering the last book added.

Actions

Identifying a resource is easy: you know how to access it and you even know how to request for a specific format (if there is more than one); but that's not all that REST proposes. Since REST is using the HTTP protocol as a standing point, the latter provides a set of verbs that can be used to reference the type of action being done over a resource.

There are other actions, aside from accessing, that a client app can take in the resources provided by an API; these depend on the service provided by the API. These actions could potentially be anything, just like the type of resources handled by the system. Still, there is a set of common actions that any system that is resource-oriented should be able to provide: CRUD (create, retrieve, update, and delete) actions.

These so-called actions can be directly mapped to the HTTP verbs, but REST does not enforce a standardized way to do so. However, there are some actions that are naturally derived by the verb and others that have been standardized by the API development community over the years, as shown in Table 1-2.

Table 1-2. *HTTP Verbs and Their Proposed Actions*

HTTP Verb	Proposed Action
GET	Access a resource in a read-only mode.
POST	Normally used to send a new resource into the server (create action).
PUT	Normally used to update a given resource (update action).
DELETE	Used to delete a resource.
HEAD	Not part of the CRUD actions, but the verb is used to ask if a given resource exists without returning any of its representations.
OPTIONS	Not part of the CRUD actions, but used to retrieve a list of available verbs on a given resource (i.e., What can the client do with a specific resource?).

That said, a client may or may not support all of these actions; it depends on what needs to be achieved. For instance, web browsers— a clear and common example of a REST client— only have support for GET and POST verbs from within the HTML code of a page, such as links and forms (although using the `XMLHTTPRequest` object from JavaScript would provide support for the major verbs mentioned earlier).

▒ **Note** The list of verbs and their corresponding actions are *suggestions*. For instance, there are some developers who prefer to switch PUT and POST, by having PUT add new elements and POST update them.

Complex Actions

CRUD actions are normally required, but they're just a very small subset of the entire spectrum of actions that a client can do with a specific resource or set of resources.

For instance, take common actions like searching, filtering, working with subresources (e.g., the books of an author, the reviews of a book, etc.), sharing a blogpost, and so forth. All of these actions fail to directly match one of the verbs that I mentioned.

The first solution that many developers succumb to is to specify the action taken as part of the URL; so you might end up with things like the following:

```
GET /api/v1/blogpost/12342/like
GET /api/v1/books/search
GET /api/v1/authors/filtering
```

Those URLs break the URI principle, because they're not referencing a unique resource at any given time; instead, they're referencing an action on a resource (or group of resources). They might seem like a good idea at first, but in the long run, and if the system keeps on growing, there will be too many URLs, which will increase the complexity of the client using the API.

So to keep things simple, use the following rule of thumb: *Hide the complexity of your actions behind the ? sign.*

This rule can apply to all verbs, not just GET, and can help achieve complex actions without compromising the URL complexity of the API. For the preceding examples, the URIs could become something like this:

```
PUT /api/v1/blogposts/12342?action=like
GET /api/v1/books?q=[SEARCH-TERM]
GET /api/v1/authors?filters=[COMMA SEPARATED LIST OF FILTERS]
```

Notice how the first one changed from a GET to a PUT due to the fact that the action is updating a resource by liking it.

Hypermedia in the Response and Main Entry Point

To make REST's interface uniform, several constraints must be applied. One of them is *Hypermedia as the Engine of Application State*, also known as *HATEOAS*. I'll go over what that concept means, how it is meant to be applied by a RESTful system, and finally, how you end up with a great new feature that allows any RESTful system client to start the interaction knowing only a single endpoint of the entire system (the root endpoint).

Again, the structure of a resource contains a section called *metadata*; inside that section, the representation of every resource should contain a set of hypermedia links that let the client know what to do with each resource. By providing this information in the response itself, the next steps any client can take are there, thus providing an even greater level of decoupling between client and server.

Changes to the resource identifiers, or added and removed functionalities, can be provided through this method without affecting the client at all, or at worst, with minimal impact.

Think of a web browser: all it needs to help a user navigate through a favorite site is the home page URL; after that, the following actions are presented inside the representation (HTML code) as links. Those are the only logical next steps that the user can take, and from there, new links will be presented, and so on.

In the case of a RESTful service, the same thing can be said: by calling upon the main endpoint (also known as *bookmark* or *root endpoint*), the client will discover all possible first steps (normally things like resource lists and other relevant endpoints).

Let's look at an example in Listing 1-1.

Root endpoint: `GET /api/v1/`

Listing 1-1. Example of a JSON Response from the Root Endpoint

```
{
  "metadata": {
    "links": [
      "books": {
        "uri": "/books",
        "content-type": "application/json"
      },
      "authors": {
        "uri": "/authors",
        "content-type": "application/json"
      }
    ]
  }
}
```

Books list endpoint: `GET /api/v1/books`

Listing 1-2. Example of Another JSON Response with Hyperlinks to Other Resources

```
{
 "resources": [
  {
   "title": "Harry Potter and the Half Blood prince",
   "description": "......",
   "author": {
    "name": "J.K.Rowling",
    "metadata": {
     "links": {
      "data": {
       "uri": "/authors/j-k-rowling",
       "content-type": "application/json"
      },
```

```
        "books": {
         "uri": "/authors/j-k-rowling/books",
         "content-type": "application/json"
        }
       }
     }
    },
    "copies": 10
   },
   {
    "title": "Dune",
    "description": "......",
    "author": {
      "name": "Frank Herbert",
      "metadata": {
        "links": {
          "data": {
            "uri": "/authors/frank-herbert",
            "content-type": "application/json"
          },
          "books": {
            "uri": "/authors/frank-herbert/books",
            "content-type": "application/json"
          }
        }
      }
    },
    "copies": 5
   }
  ],
"total": 100,
"metadata": {
  "links": {
    "next": {
      "uri": "/books?page=1",
      "content-type": "application/json"
    }
  }
 }
}
```

There are three sections highlighted in Listing 1-2; these are the links returned on the response. With that information, the client application knows the following logical steps:

1. How to get the information from the books authors
2. How to get the list of books by the authors
3. How to get the next page of results

Note that the full list of authors is not accessible through this endpoint; this is because it's not needed in this particular use case, so the API just doesn't return it. It was present on the root endpoint, though; so if the client needs it when displaying the information to the end user, it should still be available.

Each link from the preceding example contains an attribute specifying the content-type of the representation of that resource. If the resources have more than one possible representation, the different formats could be added as different links inside each resource's metadata element, letting the client choose the most adequate to the current use case, or the type could change based on the client's preferences (content negotiation).

Note that the earlier JSON structure (more specifically, the metadata elements' structure) is not important. The relevant part of the example is the information presented in the response. Each server has the freedom to design the structure as needed.

Not having a standard structure might harm the developer experience while interacting with your system, so it might be a good idea to adopt one. This is certainly not enforced by REST, but it would be a major point in favor of your system. A good standard to adopt in this case would be *Hypertext Application Language*, or HAL,[6] which tries to create a standard for both XML and JSON when representing resources with those languages.

A Few Notes on HAL

HAL tries to define a representation as having two major elements: resources and links.

According to HAL, a resource has links, embedded resources (other resources associated to their parent), and a state (the actual properties that describe the resource). On the other hand, links have a target (the URI), a relation, and some other optional properties to deal with deprecation, content negotiation, and so forth.

Listing 1-3 shows the preceding example represented using the HAL format.

Listing 1-3. JSON Response Following the HAL Standard

```
{
  "_embedded": [
    {
      "title": "Harry Potter and the Half Blood prince",
      "description": "......",
      "copies": 10,
      "_embedded": {
        "author": {
          "name": "J.K.Rowling",
          "_links": {
            "self": {
              "href": "/authors/j-k-rowling",
              "type": "application/json+hal"
            },
            "books": {
              "href": "/authors/j-k-rowling/books",
              "type": "application/json+hal"
            }
          }
        }
      }
    },
    {
      "title": "Dune",
      "description": "......",
```

[6]See http://stateless.co/hal_specification.html.

```
      "copies": 5,
      "_embedded": {
        "author": {
          "name": "Frank Herbert",
          "_links": {
            "self": {
              "href": "/authors/frank-herbert",
              "type": "application/json+hal"
            },
            "books": {
              "href": "/authors/frank-herbert/books",
              "type": "application/json+hal"
            }
          }
        }
      }
    }
  ],
  "total": 100,
  "_links": {
    "self": {
     "href": "/books",
     "type": "application/json+hal"
    },
    "next": {
      "href": "/books?page=1",
      "type": "application/json+hal"
    }
  }
}
```

The main change in Listing 1-3 is that the actual books have been moved inside an element called "_embedded", as the standard dictates, since they're actual embedded documents inside the represented resource, which is the list of books (the only property that belongs to the resource is "total", representing the total number of results). The same can be said for the authors, now inside the "_embedded" element of each book.

Status Codes

Another interesting standard that REST can benefit from when based on HTTP is the usage of HTTP status codes.[7]

A *status code* is a number that summarizes the response associated to it. There are some common ones, like 404 for "Page not found," or 200 for "OK," or the always helpful 500 for "Internal server error" (that was irony, in case it wasn't clear enough).

A status code is helpful for clients to begin interpreting the response, but in most cases, it shouldn't be a substitute for it. As the API owner, you can't really transmit in the response what exactly caused a crash on your side by just replying with the number 500. There are some cases, though, when a number is enough, like 404; although a good response will always return information that should help the client solve the problem (with a 404, a link to the home page or the root URL are good places to start).

[7]See http://www.w3.org/Protocols/rfc2616/rfc2616-sec10.html.

These codes are grouped in five sets, based on their meaning:

- *1xx*: Informational and only defined under HTTP 1.1.
- *2xx*: The request went OK, here's your content.
- *3xx*: The resource was moved somehow to somewhere.
- *4xx*: The source of the request did something wrong.
- *5xx*: The server crashed due to some error on its code.

With that in mind, Table 1-3 lists some classic status codes that an API could potentially use.

Table 1-3. *HTTP Status Codes and Their Related Interpretation*

Status Code	Meaning
200	*OK.* The request went fine and the content requested was returned. This is normally used on GET requests.
201	*Created.* The resource was created and the server has acknowledged it. It could be useful on responses to POST or PUT requests. Additionally, the new resource could be returned as part of the response body.
204	*No content.* The action was successful but there is no content returned. Useful for actions that do not require a response body, such as a DELETE action.
301	*Moved permanently.* This resource was moved to another location and the location is returned. This header is especially useful when URLs change over time (maybe due to a change on version, a migration, or some other disruptive change), keeping the old ones and returning a redirection to the new location allows old clients to update their references in their own time.
400	*Bad request.* The request issued has problems (might be lacking some required parameters, for example). A good addition to a 400 response might be an error message that a developer can use to fix the request.
401	*Unauthorized.* Especially useful for authentication when the requested resource is not accessible to the user owning the request.
403	*Forbidden.* The resource is not accessible, but unlike 401, authentication will not affect the response.
404	*Not found.* The URL provided does not identify any resource. A good addition to this response could be a set of valid URLs that the client can use to get back on track (root URL, previous URL used, etc.).
405	*Method not allowed.* The HTTP verb used on a resource is not allowed. For instance doing a PUT on a resource that is read-only.
500	*Internal server error.* A generic error code when an unexpected condition is met and the server crashes. Normally, this response is accompanied by an error message explaining what went wrong.

▒ **Note** To see the full list of HTTP status codes and their meaning, please refer to the RFC of HTTP 1.1.[8]

[8]See `http://tools.ietf.org/html/rfc7231#section-6`.

REST vs. the Past

Before REST was all cool and hip, and every business out there wanted to provide their clients with a RESTful API in their service, there were other options for developers who wanted to interconnect systems. These are still being used on old services or by services that required their specific features, but less and less so every year.

Back in the 1990s, the software industry started to think about system interoperability and how two (or more) computers could achieve it. Some solutions were born, such as COM,[9] created by Microsoft, and CORBA,[10] created by the Object Management Group. These were the first two implementations back then, but they had a major issue: they were not compatible with each other.

Other solutions arose, like RMI, but it was meant specifically for Java, which meant it was technology dependent, and hadn't really caught up with the development community.

By 1997, Microsoft decided to research solutions that would use XML as the main transport language and would allow systems to interconnect using RPC (Remote Procedure Call) over HTTP, thus achieving a somewhat technology-independent solution that would considerably simplify system interconnectivity. That research gave birth to XML-RPC around 1998.

Listing 1-4 is a classic XML-RPC request taken from Wikipedia[11]:

Listing 1-4. Example of an XML-RPC Request

```
<?xml version="1.0"?>
<methodCall>
  <methodName>examples.getStateName</methodName>
  <params>
    <param>
        <value><i4>40</i4></value>
    </param>
  </params>
</methodCall>
```

Listing 1-5 shows a possible response.

Listing 1-5. Example of an XML-RPC Response

```
<?xml version="1.0"?>
<methodResponse>
  <params>
    <param>
        <value><string>South Dakota</string></value>
    </param>
  </params>
</methodResponse>
```

From the examples shown Listing 1-4 and Listing 1-5, it is quite clear that the messages (both requests and responses) were overly verbose, something that was directly related to the use of XML. There are

---

[9]See http://www.microsoft.com/com/default.mspx.
[10]See http://www.corba.org/.
[11]See http://en.wikipedia.org/wiki/XML-RPC.

implementations of XML-RPC that exist today for several operating systems and programming languages, like Apache XML-RPC[12] (written in Java), XMLRPC-EPI[13] (written in C), and XML-RPC-C[14] for C and C++ (see Figure 1-7).

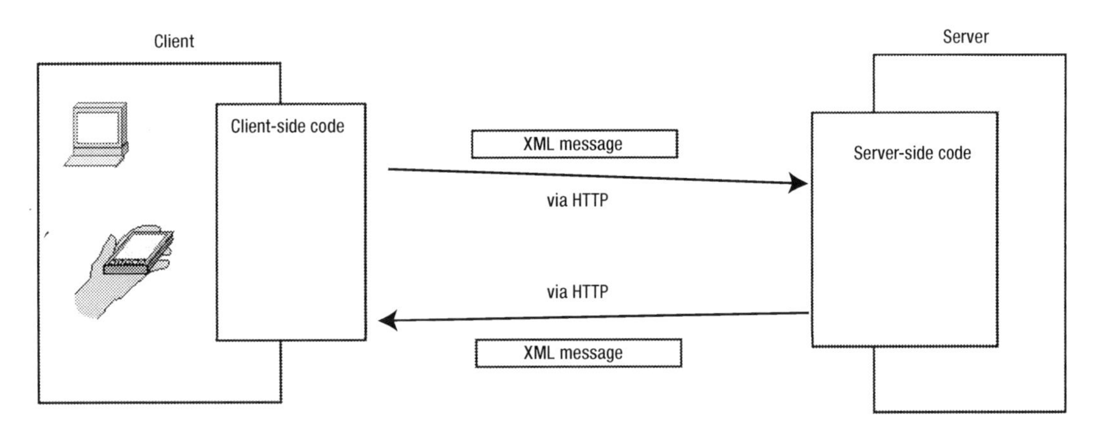

Figure 1-7. *Diagram showing the basic architecture of an XML-RPC interaction*

After XML-RPC became more popular, it mutated into SOAP,[15] a more standardized and formalized version of the same principle. SOAP still uses XML as the transport language, but the message format is now richer (and therefore complex). Listing 1-6 is an example from W3C's specification page on SOAP:

Listing 1-6. Example of a SOAP Request

```
<?xml version='1.0' ?>
<env:Envelope xmlns:env="http://www.w3.org/2003/05/soap-envelope">
 <env:Header>
  <m:reservation xmlns:m="http://travelcompany.example.org/reservation"
          env:role="http://www.w3.org/2003/05/soap-envelope/role/next"
           env:mustUnderstand="true">
   <m:reference>uuid:093a2da1-q345-739r-ba5d-pqff98fe8j7d</m:reference>
   <m:dateAndTime>2001-11-29T13:20:00.000-05:00</m:dateAndTime>
  </m:reservation>
  <n:passenger xmlns:n="http://mycompany.example.com/employees"
         env:role="http://www.w3.org/2003/05/soap-envelope/role/next"
          env:mustUnderstand="true">
   <n:name>Åke Jógvan Øyvind</n:name>
  </n:passenger>
 </env:Header>
 <env:Body>
  <p:itinerary
    xmlns:p="http://travelcompany.example.org/reservation/travel">
```

[12]See http://ws.apache.org/xmlrpc/.
[13]See http://xmlrpc-epi.sourceforge.net.
[14]See http://xmlrpc-c.sourceforge.net/.
[15]See http://www.w3.org/TR/soap/.

```
    <p:departure>
      <p:departing>New York</p:departing>
      <p:arriving>Los Angeles</p:arriving>
      <p:departureDate>2001-12-14</p:departureDate>
      <p:departureTime>late afternoon</p:departureTime>
      <p:seatPreference>aisle</p:seatPreference>
    </p:departure>
    <p:return>
      <p:departing>Los Angeles</p:departing>
      <p:arriving>New York</p:arriving>
      <p:departureDate>2001-12-20</p:departureDate>
      <p:departureTime>mid-morning</p:departureTime>
      <p:seatPreference/>
    </p:return>
  </p:itinerary>
  <q:lodging
    xmlns:q="http://travelcompany.example.org/reservation/hotels">
    <q:preference>none</q:preference>
  </q:lodging>
 </env:Body>
</env:Envelope>
```

Figure 1-8 shows the basic structure of the example from Listing 1-6.

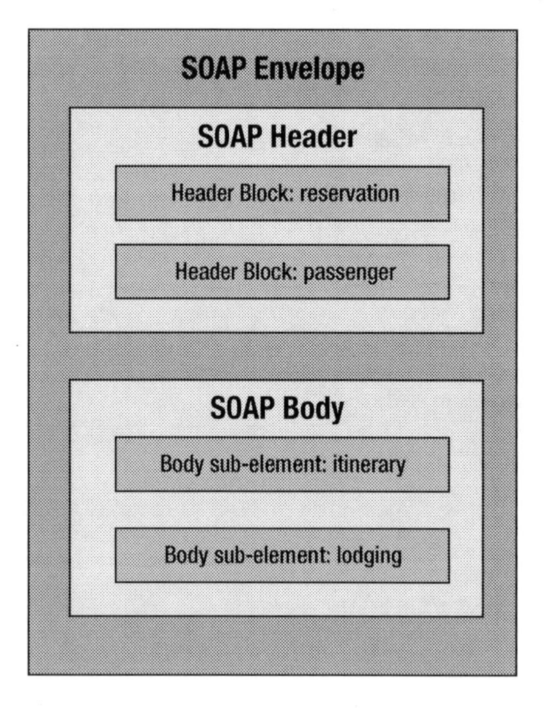

Figure 1-8. *Image from the W3C SOAP spec page*

SOAP services are actually dependent on another technology called Web Service Description Language (WSDL). An XML-based language, it describes the services provided to clients that want to consume them.

Listing 1-7 is an annotated WSDL example taken from the W3C web site.[16]

Listing 1-7. WSDL Example

```
<?xml version="1.0"?>

<!-- root element wsdl:definitions defines set of related services -->
<wsdl:definitions name="EndorsementSearch"
  targetNamespace="http://namespaces.snowboard-info.com"
  xmlns:es="http://www.snowboard-info.com/EndorsementSearch.wsdl"
  xmlns:esxsd="http://schemas.snowboard-info.com/EndorsementSearch.xsd"
  xmlns:soap="http://schemas.xmlsoap.org/wsdl/soap/"
  xmlns:wsdl="http://schemas.xmlsoap.org/wsdl/">

  <!-- wsdl:types encapsulates schema definitions of communication types; here using xsd -->
  <wsdl:types>

    <!-- all type declarations are in a chunk of xsd -->
    <xsd:schema targetNamespace="http://namespaces.snowboard-info.com"
     xmlns:xsd="http://www.w3.org/1999/XMLSchema">

      <!-- xsd definition: GetEndorsingBoarder [manufacturer string, model string] -->
      <xsd:element name="GetEndorsingBoarder">
        <xsd:complexType>
          <xsd:sequence>
            <xsd:element name="manufacturer" type="string"/>
            <xsd:element name="model" type="string"/>
          </xsd:sequence>
        </xsd:complexType>
      </xsd:element>

      <!-- xsd definition: GetEndorsingBoarderResponse [...endorsingBoarder string...] -->
      <xsd:element name="GetEndorsingBoarderResponse">
        <xsd:complexType>
          <xsd:all>
            <xsd:element name="endorsingBoarder" type="string"/>
          </xsd:all>
        </xsd:complexType>
      </xsd:element>

      <!-- xsd definition: GetEndorsingBoarderFault [...errorMessage string...] -->
      <xsd:element name="GetEndorsingBoarderFault">
        <xsd:complexType>
          <xsd:all>
            <xsd:element name="errorMessage" type="string"/>
          </xsd:all>
```

[16]See http://www.w3.org/2001/03/14-annotated-WSDL-examples.

```
        </xsd:complexType>
      </xsd:element>

    </xsd:schema>
  </wsdl:types>

  <!-- wsdl:message elements describe potential transactions -->

  <!-- request GetEndorsingBoarderRequest is of type GetEndorsingBoarder -->

  <wsdl:message name="GetEndorsingBoarderRequest">
    <wsdl:part name="body" element="esxsd:GetEndorsingBoarder"/>
  </wsdl:message>

  <!-- response GetEndorsingBoarderResponse is of type GetEndorsingBoarderResponse -->
  <wsdl:message name="GetEndorsingBoarderResponse">
    <wsdl:part name="body" element="esxsd:GetEndorsingBoarderResponse"/>
  </wsdl:message>

  <!-- wsdl:portType describes messages in an operation -->
  <wsdl:portType name="GetEndorsingBoarderPortType">

    <!-- the value of wsdl:operation eludes me -->
    <wsdl:operation name="GetEndorsingBoarder">
      <wsdl:input message="es:GetEndorsingBoarderRequest"/>
      <wsdl:output message="es:GetEndorsingBoarderResponse"/>
      <wsdl:fault message="es:GetEndorsingBoarderFault"/>
    </wsdl:operation>
  </wsdl:portType>

  <!-- wsdl:binding states a serialization protocol for this service -->
  <wsdl:binding name="EndorsementSearchSoapBinding"
                type="es:GetEndorsingBoarderPortType">

    <!-- leverage off soap:binding document style @@@(no wsdl:foo pointing at the soap
     binding) -->
    <soap:binding style="document"
              transport="http://schemas.xmlsoap.org/soap/http"/>

    <!-- semi-opaque container of network transport details classed by soap:binding
     above @@@ -->
    <wsdl:operation name="GetEndorsingBoarder">

      <!-- again bind to SOAP? @@@ -->
      <soap:operation soapAction="http://www.snowboard-info.com/EndorsementSearch"/>

      <!-- furthur specify that the messages in the wsdl:operation "GetEndorsingBoarder"
       use SOAP? @@@ -->
      <wsdl:input>
        <soap:body use="literal"
                   namespace="http://schemas.snowboard-info.com/EndorsementSearch.xsd"/>
      </wsdl:input>
      <wsdl:output>
        <soap:body use="literal"
                   namespace="http://schemas.snowboard-info.com/EndorsementSearch.xsd"/>
      </wsdl:output>
      <wsdl:fault>
```

```
        <soap:body use="literal"
                   namespace="http://schemas.snowboard-info.com/EndorsementSearch.xsd"/>
      </wsdl:fault>
    </wsdl:operation>
  </wsdl:binding>

    <!-- wsdl:service names a new service "EndorsementSearchService" -->
    <wsdl:service name="EndorsementSearchService">
    <wsdl:documentation>snowboarding-info.com Endorsement Service
    </wsdl:documentation>

    <!-- connect it to the binding "EndorsementSearchSoapBinding" above -->
    <wsdl:port name="GetEndorsingBoarderPort"
               binding="es:EndorsementSearchSoapBinding">

      <!-- give the binding an network address -->
      <soap:address location="http://www.snowboard-info.com/EndorsementSearch"/>
    </wsdl:port>
  </wsdl:service>

</wsdl:definitions>
```

The main drawback of these types of services was the amount of information used, both to describe them and to use them. Even though XML provided the much-required technology agnostic means of encoding data to be transmitted between two systems, it also blotted the message sent quite noticeably.

Both of these technologies (XML-RPC and SOAP + WSDL) provided the solution to system interconnectivity at a time when it was required. They provided a way to transmit messages using a "universal" language between all systems, but they also had several major issues compared to today's leading standard (see Table 1-4). This can be clearly seen, for example, in the way developers feel about using XML instead of JSON.

Table 1-4. *Comparison of XML-RPC/SOAP and REST Services*

XML-RCP / SOAP	REST
Specific SOAP clients had to be created for each programming language. Even though XML was universal, a new client would have to be coded to parse the WSDL to understand how the service worked.	REST is completely technology agnostic and doesn't require special clients, only a programming language capable of connectivity through the chosen protocol (e.g., HTTP, FTP, etc.).
The client needs to know everything about the service before initiating the interaction (thus the WSDL mentioned earlier).	The client only needs to know the main root endpoint, and with the hypermedia provided on the response, self-discovery is possible.
Because the service was used from within the client source code and called a specific function or method from within the server's code, the coupling between those two systems was too big. A rewrite of the server code would probably lead to a rewrite on the client's code.	The interface is implementation independent; the complete server-side code can be rewritten and the API's interface will not have to be changed.

▒ **Note** Comparing XML-RPC/SOAP with REST might not be entirely fair (or possible) due to the fact that the first two are protocols, whereas the latter is an architectural style; but some points can still be compared if you keep that distinction in mind.

Summary

This chapter was a small overview of what REST is meant to be and what kind of benefits a system will gain by following the REST style. The chapter also covered a few extra principles, like HTTP verbs and status codes, which although are not part of the REST style, are indeed part of the HTTP standard, the protocol we're basing this book on.

Finally, I discussed the main technologies used prior to REST, and you saw how they compared to the current leading industry standard.

In the next chapter, I'll go over some good API design practices and you'll see how you can achieve them using REST.

CHAPTER 2

API Design Best Practices

The practice of API design is a tricky one. Even when there are so many options out there—tools to use, standards to apply, styles to follow—there is one basic question that needs to be answered and needs to be clear in the developer's mind before any kind design and development can begin...

What Defines a Good API?

As we all know, the concepts of "good" and "bad" are very subjective (one could probably read a couple of books discussing this on its own), and therefore, opinions vary from one person to another. That being said, years of experience of dealing with different kinds of APIs have left the developer community (and this author) with a pretty good sense of the need-to-have features of any good API. (Disclaimer: Things like clean code, good development practices, and other internal considerations will not be mentioned here, but will be assumed, since they should be part of every software undertaking.)

So let's go over this list.

- *Developer friendly*: The developers working with your API should not suffer when dealing with your system.
- *Extensibility*: Your system should be able to handle the addition of new features without breaking your clients.
- *Up-to-date documentation*: Good documentation is key to your API being picked up by new developers.
- *Proper error handling*: Because things will go wrong and you need to be prepared.
- *Provides multiple SDK/libraries*: The more work you simplify for developers, the more they'll like your system.
- *Security*: A key aspect of any global system.
- *Scalability*: The ability to scale up and down is something any good API should have to properly provide its services.

I'll go over these points one by one and show how they affect the API, and how following the REST style help.

Developer Friendly

By definition, an API is an *application programming interface*, with the key word being *interface*. When thinking about designing an API that will be used by developers other than yourself, there is a key aspect that needs to be taken into consideration: the Developer eXperience (or DX).

F. Doglio, *Pro REST API Development with Node.js*, DOI 10.1007/978-1-4842-0917-2_2

Even when the API will be used by another system, the integration into that system is first done by one or more developers—human beings that bring the human factor into that integration. This means you'll want the API to be as easy to use as possible, which makes for a great DX, and which should translate into more developers and client applications using the API.

There is a trade-off, though, since simplifying things for humans could lead into an oversimplification of the interface, which in turn could lead to design issues when dealing with complex functionalities.

It is important to consider the DX as one of the major aspects of an API (let's be honest, without developers using it, there is no point to an API), but there are other aspects that have to be taken into consideration and have weight in the design decisions. *Make it simple, but not dummy simple.*

The next sections provide some pointers for a good DX.

Communication's Protocol

This is one of the most basic aspects of the interface. When choosing a communication protocol, it's always a good idea to go with one that is familiar to the developers using the API. There are several standards that already have libraries and modules available in many programming languages (e.g., HTTP, FTP, SSH, etc.).

A custom-made protocol isn't always a good idea because you'll lose that instant portability in so many existing technologies. That said, if you're ready to create support libraries for the most used languages, and your custom protocol is more efficient for your use case, it could be the right choice.

In the end, it's up to the API designer to evaluate the best solution based on the context he's working in.

In this book, you're working under the assumption that the protocol chosen for REST is HTTP.[1] It's a very well-known protocol; any modern programming language supports it and it's the basis for the entire Internet. You can rest assured that most developers have a basic understanding of how to use it. And if not, there is plenty of information out there to get to know it better.

In summary, there is no silver bullet protocol out there perfect for every scenario. Think about your API needs, make sure that whatever you choose is compatible with REST, and you'll be fine.

Easy-to-Remember Access Points

The points of contact between all client apps and the API are called *endpoints*. The API needs to provide them to allow clients to access its functionalities. This can be done through whatever communications protocol is chosen. These access points should have mnemotechnic names to help the developer understand their purpose just by reading them.

Of course, the name by itself should never be a replacement for a detailed documentation, but it is normally considered a good idea to reference the resource being used, and to have some kind of indicator of the action being taken when calling that access point.

The following is a good example of a badly named access point (meant to list the books in a bookstore):

```
GET /books/action1
```

This example uses the HTTP protocol to specify the access point, and even though the entity used (books) is being referenced, the action name is not clear; `action1` could mean anything, or even worst, the meaning could change in the future, but the name would still be suitable, so any existing client would undoubtedly break.

A better example—one that follows REST and the standards discussed in Chapter 1—would be this:

```
GET /books
```

[1]See `http://www.w3.org/Protocols/rfc2616/rfc2616.html`.

This should present the developer with more than enough information to understand that a GET request into the root of a resource (`/books`) will always yield a list of items of this type; then the developer can replicate this pattern into other resources, as long as the interface is kept uniform across all other endpoints.

Uniform Interface

Easy-to-remember access points are important, but so is being consistent when defining them. Again, you have to go back to the human factor when consuming an API: you have it. So making their lives easier is a must if you want anyone to use it, you can't forget about the DX. That means you need to be consistent when defining endpoints' names, request formats, and response formats. There can be more than one for the latter two (more specifically, the response format is directly tied to the various representations a resource can have), but as long as the default is always the same, there will be no problems.

A good example of an inconsistent interface, even though not on an API, can be seen in the programming language PHP. It has underscore notation on most functions' names, but the underscore is not used on some, so the developer is always forced to go back to the documentation to check how to write these functions (or worst, rely on his/her memory).

For example, `str_replace` is a function that uses an underscore to separate both words (`str` and `replace`), whereas `htmlentities` has no separation of words at all.

Another example of bad design practice in an API is to name the endpoints based on the actions taken instead of the resources handled; for example:

```
/getAllBooks
/submitNewBook
/updateAuthor
/getBooksAuthors
/getNumberOfBooksOnStock
```

These examples clearly show the pattern that this API is following. And at a first glance, they might not seem that bad, but consider how poor the interface is going to become as new features and resources are added to the system (not to mention if the actions are modified). Each new addition to the system causes extra endpoints to the API's interface. The developers of client apps will have no clue as to how these new endpoints are named. For instance, if the API is extended to support the cover images of books, with the current naming scheme, these are all possible new endpoints:

```
/addNewImageToBook
/getBooksImages
/addCoverImage
/listBooksCovers
```

And the list can go on. So for any real-world application, you can safely assume that following this type of pattern will yield a really big list of endpoints, increasing the complexity of both server-side code and client-side code. It will also hurt the system's ability to capture new developers, due to the inherited complexity that it will have over the years.

To solve this problem, and generate an easy-to-use and uniform interface across the entire API, you can apply the REST style to the endpoints. If you remember the constraints proposed by REST from Chapter 1, you end up with a resource-centric interface. And thanks to HTTP, you also have verbs to indicate actions.

Table 2-1 shows how the previous interface changes using REST.

Table 2-1. *List of Endpoints and How They Change When the REST Style Is Applied*

Old Style	REST Style
/getAllBooks	GET /books
/submitNewBook	POST /books
/updateAuthor	PUT /authors/:id
/getBooksAuthors	GET /books/:id/authors
/getNumberOfBooksOnStock	GET /books (This number can easily be returned as part of this endpoint.)
/addNewImageToBook	PUT /books/:id
/getBooksImages	GET /books/:id/images
/addCoverImage	POST /books/:id/cover_image
/listBooksCovers	GET /books (This information can be returned in this endpoint using subresources.)

You went from having to remember nine different endpoints to just two, with the added bonus of having all HTTP verbs being the same in all cases once you defined the standard; now there is no need to remember specific roles in each case (they'll always mean the same thing).

Transport Language

Another aspect of the interface to consider is the *transport language* used. For many years, the de facto standard was XML; it provided a technology-agnostic way of expressing data that could easily be sent between clients and servers. Nowadays, there is a new standard gaining popularity over XML—JSON.

Why JSON?

JSON has been gaining traction over the past few years (see Figure 2-1) as the standard Data Transfer Format. This is mainly due to the advantages that it provides. The following lists just a few:

- It's lightweight. There is very little data in a JSON file that is not directly related to the information being transferred. This is a major winning point over more verbose formats like XML.[2]
- It's human readable. The format itself is so simple that it can easily be read and written by a human. This is particularly important considering that a focus point of the interface of any good API is the human factor (otherwise known as the DX).
- It supports different data types. Because not everything being transferred is a string, this feature allows the developer to provide extra meaning to the information transferred.

[2] XML is not strictly a Data Transfer Format, but it's being used as one.

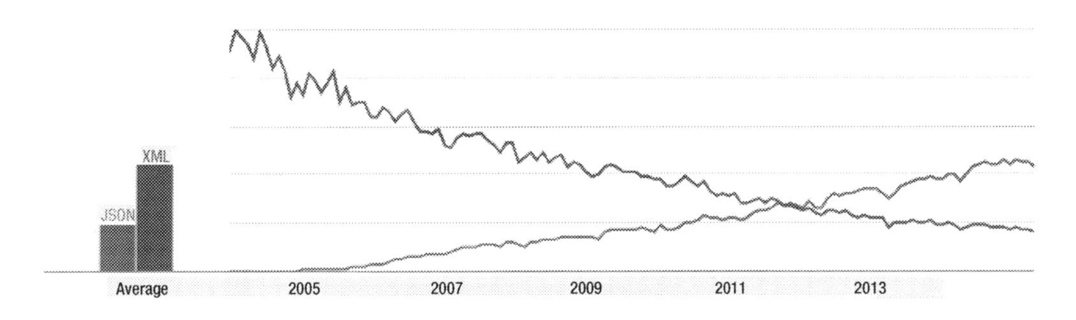

Figure 2-1. *Trend of Google searches for "JSON" vs. "XML" over the last few years*

The list could go on, but these are the three main aspects that are helping JSON win so many followers in the developer community.

Even though JSON is a great format and is gaining traction, it's not the silver bullet that will always solve all of your problems; so it's also important to provide clients with options. And here is where REST comes to help.

Since the protocol you're basing REST on is HTTP, developers can use a mechanism called *content negotiation* to allow clients to specify which of the supported formats they want to receive (as discussed in Chapter 1). This allows for more flexibility on the API, and still keeps the interface uniform.

Going back to the list of endpoints, the last one talks about using a subresource as the solution. That can be interpreted in several ways, because not only is the language used to transfer the data important, but so is the structure that you give the data being transferred. My final advice for a uniform interface is to standardize the format used, or even better, follow an existing one, like HAL.

This was covered in the previous chapter, so refer back to it for more information.

Extensibility

A good API is never fully finished. This might be a bold claim, but it's one that comes from the experience of the community. Let's look at some of the big ones.[3]

- Google APIs - 5 billion calls a day[4]; launched in 2005
- Facebook APIs - 5 billion calls a day[5]; launched in 2007
- Twitter APIs - 13 billion calls a day[6]; launched in 2006

These examples show that even when a great team is behind the API, the APIs will keep growing and changing because the client apps developers find new ways to use it, the business model of the API owner changes over time, or simply because features are added and removed.

When any of this happens, the API may need to be extended or changed, and new access points added or old ones changed. If the original design is right, then going from v1 to v2 should be no problem, but if it's not, then that migration could spell disaster for everyone.

[3]Source: `http://www.slideshare.net/3scale/apis-for-biz-dev-20-which-business-model-15473323`.
[4]April 2010.
[5]October 2009.
[6]May 2011.

How Is Extensibility Managed?

When extending the API, you're basically releasing a new version of your software, so the first thing you need to do is let your users (the developers) know what will happen once the new version is out. Will their apps still work? Are the changes backward-compatible? Will you maintain several versions of your API online, or just the latest one?

A good API should take the following points into consideration:

- How easily can new endpoints be added?
- Is the new version backward-compatible?
- Can clients continue to work with older versions of the API while their code is being updated?
- What will happen to existing clients targeting the new API?
- How easy will it be for clients to target the new version of the API?

Once all these points are settled, then you can safely grow and extend the API .

Normally, going from version A to version B of an API by instantly deprecating version A and taking it offline in favor of version B is considered a bad move, unless you have very few client applications using that version, of course.

A better approach for this type of situation is to allow developers to choose which version of the API they want to use, keeping the old version long enough to let everyone migrate into the newer one. And in order to do this, an API would include its version number in the resource identifier (i.e., the URL of each resource). This approach makes the version number a mandatory part of the URL to clearly show the version in use.

Another approach, which may not be as clear, is to provide a versionless URL that points to the latest version of the API, and an optional URL parameter to overwrite the version. Both approaches have pros and cons that have to be weighted by the developer creating the API.

Table 2-2. *Pros and Cons of Having the Version of the API As Part of the URL*

Pros	Cons
The version number is clearly visible, helping avoid confusion about the version being used.	URLs are more verbose.
Easy to migrate from one version to another, from a client perspective (all URLs change the same portion—the version number)	A wrong implementation on the API code could cause a huge amount of work when migrating from one version to the other (i.e., if the version is hardcoded on the endpoint's URL template, individually for every endpoint).
Allows cleaner architecture when more than one version of the API needs to be kept working.	
Clear and simple migration from one version to the next from the API perspective, since both versions could be kept working in parallel for a period of time, allowing slower clients to migrate without breaking.	
The right versioning scheme can make fixes and backward-compatible new features instantly available without the need to update on the client's part.	

Table 2-3. Pros and Cons of Having the API Version Hidden from the User

Pros	Cons
Simpler URLs.	A Hidden version number might lead to confusion about the version being used.
Instant migration to latest working code of the API.	Non-backward-compatible changes will break the clients that are not referencing a specific version of the API.
Simple migration from one version to the next from the client's perspective (only change the value of the attribute).	Complex architecture required to make version selection available.
Easy test of client code against the latest version (just don't send version-specific parameters).	

Keeping this in mind, there are several versioning schemes to use when it comes to setting the version of a software product:

Ubuntu's[7] version numbers represent the year and month of the release; so version 14.04 means it was released in April 2014.

In the Chromium project, version numbers have four parts[8]: MAJOR.MINOR.BUILD.PATCH. The following is from the Chromium project's page on versioning: MAJOR and MINOR *may* get updated with any significant Google Chrome release (Beta or Stable update). MAJOR *must* get updated for any backward-incompatible user data change (since this data survives updates). BUILD *must* get updated whenever a release candidate is built from the current trunk (at least weekly for Dev channel release candidates). The BUILD number is an ever-increasing number representing a point in time of the Chromium trunk. PATCH *must* get updated whenever a release candidate is built from the BUILD branch.

Another intermediate approach, known as Semantic Versioning or SemVer,[9] is well accepted by the community. It provides the right amount of information. It has three numbers for each version: MAJOR.MINOR.PATCH.

- MAJOR represents changes that are not backward-compatible.
- MINOR represents new features that leave the API backward-compatible.
- PATCH represents small changes like bug fixes and code optimization.

With that scheme, the first number is the only one that is really relevant to clients, since that'll be the one indicating compatibility with their current version.

By having the latest version of MINOR and PATCH deployed on the API at all times, you're providing clients with the latest compatible features and bug fixes, without making clients update their code.

So with that simple versioning scheme, the endpoints look like this:

```
GET /1/books?limit=10&size=10
POST /v2/photos
GET /books?v=1
```

[7]See `https://help.ubuntu.com/community/CommonQuestions#Ubuntu_Releases_and_Version_Numbers`.
[8]See `http://www.chromium.org/developers/version-numbers`.
[9]See semver.org.

When choosing a versioning scheme, please take the following into consideration:

- Using the wrong versioning scheme might cause confusion or problems when implementing a client app, by consuming the wrong version of the API. For instance, using Ubuntu's versioning scheme for your API might not be the best way to communicate what is going on in each new version.
- The wrong versioning scheme might force clients to update a lot, like when a minor fix is deployed or a new backward-compatible feature is added. Those changes shouldn't require a client update. So don't force the client to specify those parts of the version unless your scheme requires it.

Up-to-Date Documentation

No matter how mnemotechnic your endpoints are, you still need to have documentation explaining everything that your API does. Whether optional parameters or the mechanics of an access point, the documentation is fundamental to having a good DX, which translates into more users.

A good API requires more than just a few lines explaining how to use an access point (there is nothing worse than discovering that you need an access point but it has no documentation at all), but needs a full list of parameters and explanatory examples.

Some providers give developers a simple web interface to try their API without having to write any code. This is particularly useful for newcomers.

There are some online services that allow API developers to upload their documentation, as well as those that provide the web UI to test the API; for example, Mashape provides this service for free (see Figure 2-2).

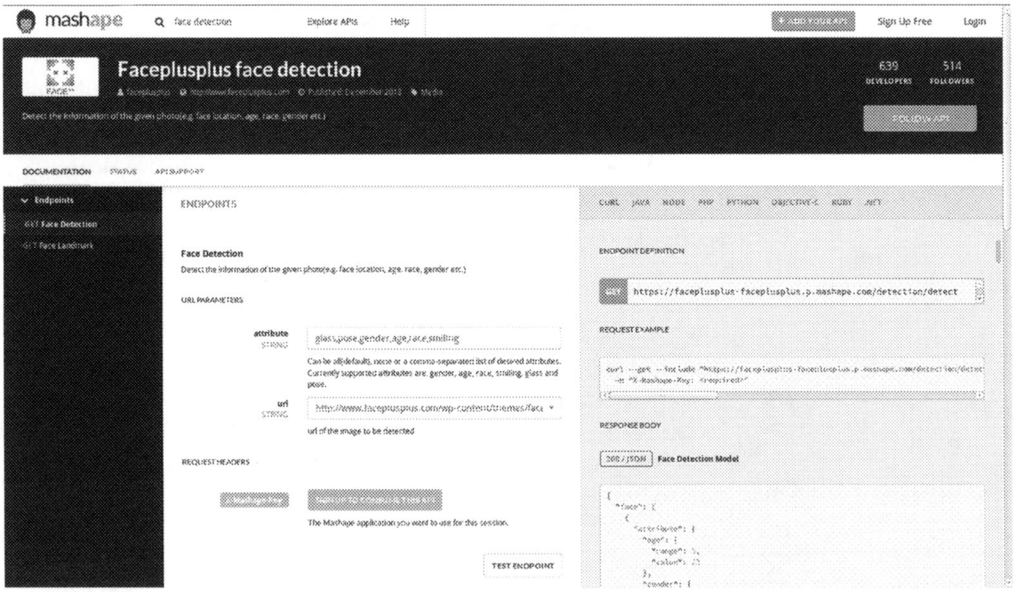

Figure 2-2. *The service provided by Mashape*

Another good example of detailed documentation is at Facebook's developer site.[10] It provides implementation and usage examples for all the platforms that Facebook supports (see Figure 2-3).

[10] See `https://developers.facebook.com/docs/graph-api/using-graph-api/v2.1`.

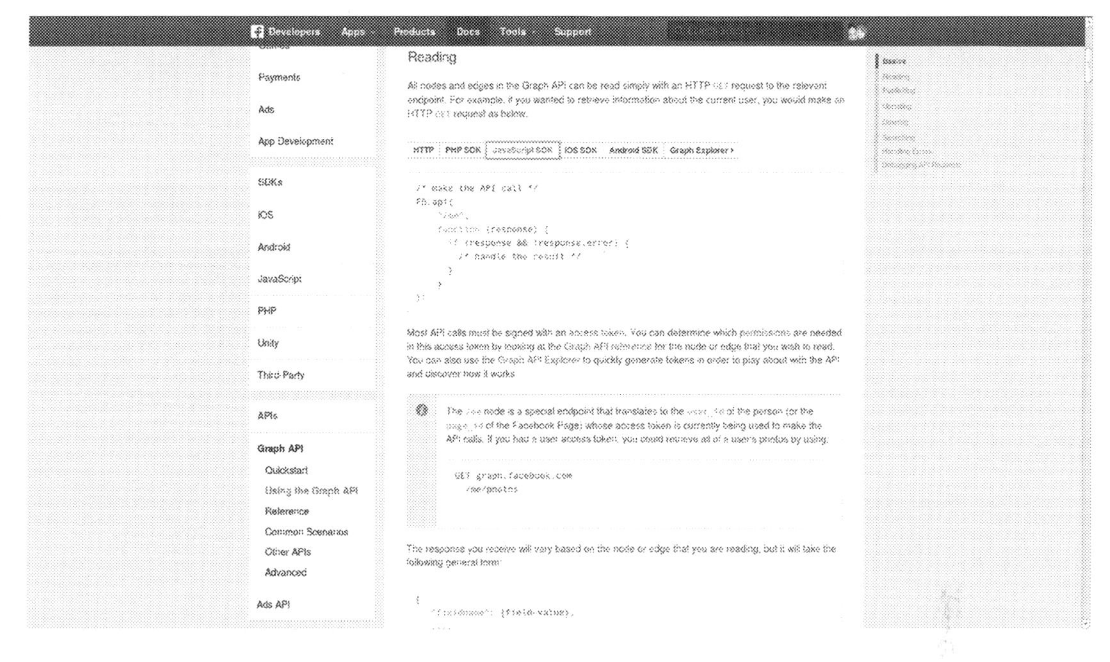

***Figure 2-3.** Facebook's API documentation site*

An example of a poorly written documentation is seen in Figure 2-4. It is 4chan's API documentation.[11]

README.md

4chan API

Welcome

Welcome to 4chan's read-only JSON API documentation

JSON representations of threads and indexes are exposed at the following URLs:

http(s)://a.4cdn.org/ board /thread/ threadnumber .json
http(s)://a.4cdn.org/ board / pagenumber .json (1 is main index)

A JSON representation of all thread OPs (and the replies shown on indexes) from an individual board can be found at the following URL.

http(s)://a.4cdn.org/ board /catalog.json

And just the thread IDs, their modification times, and respective pages can be found here.

http(s)://a.4cdn.org/ board /threads.json

A list of boards is exposed at the following URL:

http(s)://a.4cdn.org/boards.json

CORS is supported with an origin of http(s)://boards.4chan.org

Supported request methods are: GET, HEAD, OPTIONS

Questions? Please e-mail

This guide was last updated August 12, 2014.

API Rules

1. Do not make more than one request per second.

***Figure 2-4.** Introduction to 4chan's API documentation*

[11] See `https://github.com/4chan/4chan-API`.

Yes, the API appears to not be complicated enough to merit writing a whole book about it, but then again, there are no examples provided, only a generic explanation of how to find the endpoints and what parameters to use.

Newcomers might find it hard to understand how to implement a simple client that uses this API.

▒ **Note** It's unfair to compare 4chan's documentation to that of Facebook's, since the size of the teams and companies are completely different. But you should note the lack of quality in 4chan's documentation.

Although it might not seem like the most productive idea while developing an API, the team needs to consider working on extensive documentation. It is one of the main things that will assure the success or failure of the API for two main reasons:

- It should help newcomers and advance developers to consume your API without any problems.
- It should serve as a blueprint for the development team, if it is kept up-to-date. Jumping into a project mid-development is easier if there is a well-written and well-explained blueprint of how the API is meant to work.

▒ **Note** This also applies to updating the documentation when changes are made to the API. You need to keep it updated; otherwise, the effect is the same as not having documentation at all.

Proper Error Handling

Error handling on an API is incredibly important, because if it is done right, it can help the client app understand how to handle errors; and on the human side of it (the DX), it can help developers understand what it is they're doing wrong and how to fix it.

There are two very distinct moments during the life cycle of an API client that you need to consider error handling:

- *Phase 1*: The development of the client.
- *Phase 2*: The client is implemented and being used by end users.

Phase 1: Development of the Client

During the first phase, developers implement the required code to consume the API. It is very likely that a developer will have errors on the requests (things like missing parameters, wrong endpoint names, etc.) during this stage.

Those errors need to be handled properly, which means returning enough information to let developers know what they did wrong and how they can fix it.

A common problem with some systems is that their creators ignore this stage, and when there is a problem with the request, the API crashes, and the returned information is just an error message with the stack trace and the status code 500.

The response in Figure 2-5 shows what happens when you forget to add error handling in the client development stage. The stack trace returned might give the developer some sort of clue (at best) as to what exactly went wrong, but it also shows a lot of unnecessary information, so it ends up being confusing. This certainly hurts development time, and no doubt would be a major point against the DX of the API.

```
{
    error: "TypeError: Cannot read property 'query' of undefined at BooksHdlr.index
    (/home/fernando/workspace/github/api-design/./handlers/books.js:20:22) at
    ProcessingChain.runChain (/home/fernando/workspace/github/api-
    design/node_modules/vatican/lib/processingChain.js:76:13) at
    /home/fernando/workspace/github/api-
    design/node_modules/vatican/lib/vatican.js:162:36 at
    /home/fernando/workspace/github/api-
    design/node_modules/vatican/lib/defaultRequestParser.js:63:13 at
    Object.module.exports.getBodyContent (/home/fernando/workspace/github/api-
    design/node_modules/vatican/lib/defaultRequestParser.js:20:13) at
    Object.module.exports.parse (/home/fernando/workspace/github/api-
    design/node_modules/vatican/lib/defaultRequestParser.js:57:14) at
    Vatican.parseRequest (/home/fernando/workspace/github/api-
    design/node_modules/vatican/lib/vatican.js:82:24) at Vatican.requestHandler
    (/home/fernando/workspace/github/api-
    design/node_modules/vatican/lib/vatican.js:154:18) at Server.EventEmitter.emit
    (events.js:98:17) at HTTPParser.parser.onIncoming (http.js:2108:12)"
}
```

Figure 2-5. A classic example of a crash on the API returning the stack trace

On the other hand, let's take a look at a proper error response for the same error in Figure 2-6.

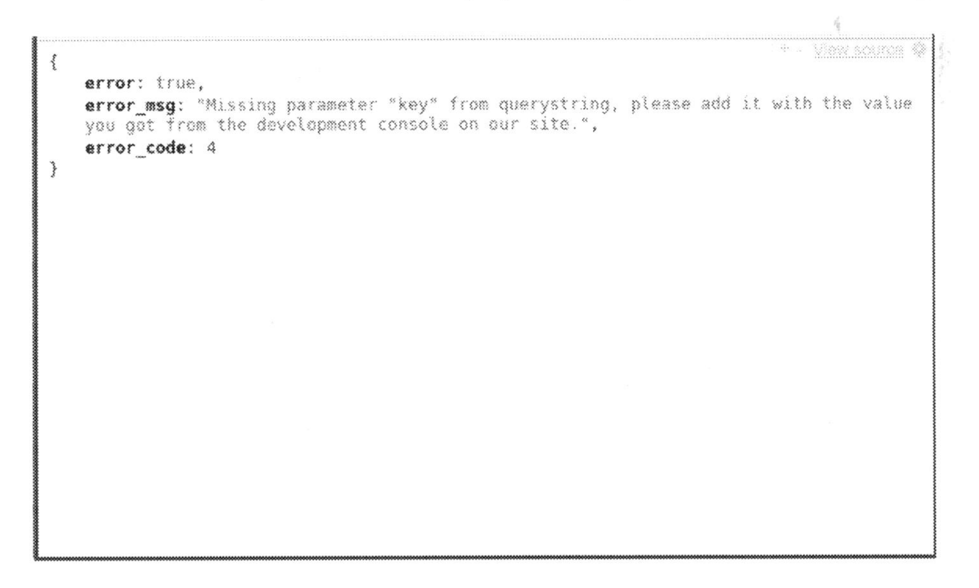

```
{
    error: true,
    error_msg: "Missing parameter "key" from querystring, please add it with the value
    you got from the development console on our site.",
    error_code: 4
}
```

Figure 2-6. A proper error response would look like this

Figure 2-6 clearly shows that there has been an error, what the error is, and an error code. The response only has three attributes, but they're all helpful:

- The error indicator gives the developer a clear way to check whether or not the response is an error message (you could also check against the status code of the response).
- The error message is clearly intended for the developer, and not only states what's missing, but also explains how to fix it.
- A custom error code, if explained in the documentation, could help a developer automate actions when this type of response happens again.

Phase 2: The Client Is Implemented and Being Used by End Users

During this stage in the life cycle of the client, you're not expecting any more developer errors, such as using the wrong endpoint, missing parameters, and the like, but there could still be problems caused by the data generated by the user.

Client applications that request some kind of input from the user are always subject to errors on the user's part, and even though there are always ways to validate that input before it reaches the API layer, it's not safe to assume all clients will do that. So the safest bet for any API designer and developer is to assume there is no validation done by the client, and anything that could go wrong, will go wrong with the data. This is also a safe assumption to make from a security point of view, so it's providing a minor security improvement as a side effect.

With that mindset, the API implemented should be rock-solid and able to handle any type of errors in the input data.

The response should mimic the one from phase 1: there should be an error indicator, an error message stating what's wrong (and if possible, how to fix it), and a custom error code. The custom error code is especially useful in this stage, since it'll provide the client with the ability to customize the error shown to the end user (even showing a different but still relevant error message).

Multiple SDK/Libraries

If you expect your API to be massively used across different technologies and platforms, it might be a good idea to develop and provide support for libraries and SDKs that can be used with your system.

By doing so, you provide developers with the means to consume your services, so all they have to do is use them to create their client apps. Essentially, you're shaving off potential weeks or months (depending on the size of your system) of development time.

Another benefit is that most developers will inherently trust your libraries over others that do the same, because you're the owner of the service those libraries are consuming.

Finally, consider open sourcing the code of your libraries. These days, the open source community is thriving. Developers will undoubtedly help maintain and improve your libraries if they're of use to them.

Let's look again at some of the biggest APIs out there:

- Facebook API provides SDKs for iOS, Android, JavaScript, PHP, and Unity.[12]
- Google Maps API provides SDKs for several technologies, including iOS, the Web, and Android.[13]

[12]See `https://developers.facebook.com` (see the bottom of the page for the list of SDKs).
[13]See `https://developers.google.com/maps/`.

- Twitter API provides SDKs for several of their APIs, including Java, ASP, C++, Clojure, .NET, Go, JavaScript, and a lot of other languages.[14]
- Amazon provides SDKs for their AWS service, including PHP, Ruby, .NET, and iOS. They even have those SDKs on GitHub for anyone to see.[15]

Security

Securing your API is a very important step in the development process and it should not be ignored, unless what you're building is small enough and has no sensitive data to merit the effort.

There are two big security issues to deal with when designing an API:

- *Authentication*: Who's going to access the API?
- *Authorization*: What will they be able to access once logged in?

Authentication deals with letting valid users access the features provided by the API. Authorization deals with handling what those authenticated users can actually do inside the system.

Before going into details about each specific issue, there are some common aspects that need to be remembered when dealing with security on RESTful systems (at least, those based on HTTP):

- *RESTful systems are meant to be stateless.* Remember that REST defines the server as stateless, which means that storing the user data in session after the initial login is not a good idea (if you want to stay within the guidelines provided by REST that is).
- *Remember to use HTTPS.* On RESTful systems based on HTTP, HTTPS should be used to assure encryption of the channel, making it harder to capture and read data traffic (man-in-the-middle attack).

Accessing the System

There are some widely used authentication schemes out there meant to provide different levels of security when signing users into a system. Some of the most commonly known ones are Basic Auth with TSL, Digest Auth, OAuth 1.0a, and OAuth 2.0.

I'll go over these and talk about each of their pros and cons. I'll also cover an alternative method that should prove to be the most RESTful, in the sense that it's 100% stateless.

Almost Stateless Methods

OAuth 1.0a, OAuth 2.0, Digest Auth, and Basic Auth + TSL are the go-to methods of authentication these days. They work wonderfully, they have been implemented in all of the modern programming languages, and they have proven to be the right choice for the job (when used for the right use-case). That being said, as you're about to see, none of them are 100% stateless.

They all depend on having the user have information stored on some kind of cache layer on the server side. This little detail, especially for the purists out there, means a no-go when designing a RESTful system, because it goes against one of the most basic of the constraints imposed by REST: *Communication between client and server must be stateless.*

---

[14]See `https://dev.twitter.com/overview/api/twitter-libraries`.
[15]See `https://github.com/aws`.

This means the state of the user should not be stored anywhere.

You will look the other way in this particular case, however. I'll cover the basics of each method anyway, because in real life, you have to compromise and you have to find a balance between purism and practicality. But don't worry. I'll go over an alternative design that will solve authentication and stay true to REST.

Basic Auth with TSL

Thanks to the fact that you're basing REST on HTTP for the purpose of this book, the latter provides a basic authentication method that most of the languages have support for.

Keep in mind, though, that this method is aptly named, since it's quite basic and works by sending the username and password unencrypted over HTTP. So the only way to make it secure is to use it with a secured connection over HTTPS (HTTP + TSL).

This authentication method works as follows (see Figure 2-7):

1. First, a client makes a request for a resource without any special header.
2. The server responds with a 401 unauthorized response, and within it, a WWW-Authenticate header, specifying the method to use (Basic or Digest) and the realm name.
3. The client then sends the same request, but adds the Authorization header, with the string USERNAME:PASSWORD encoded in base 64.

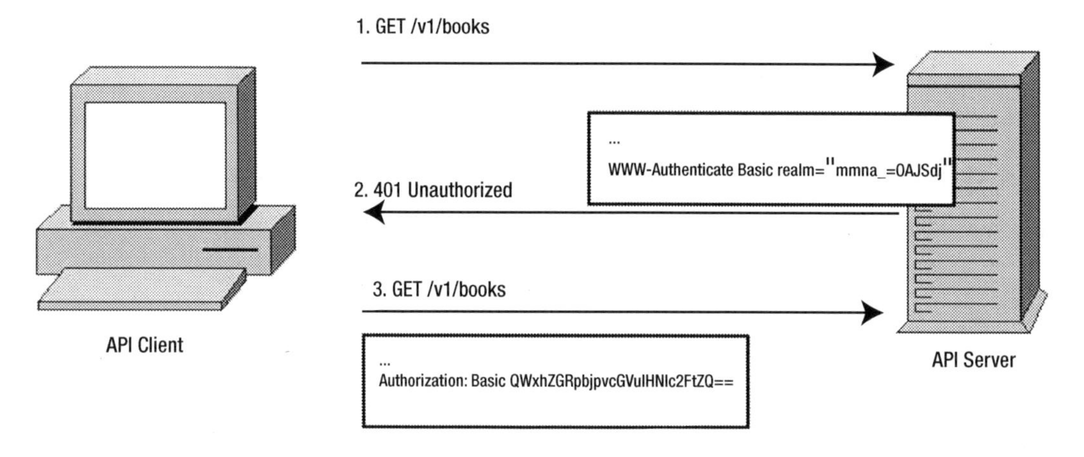

Figure 2-7. *The steps between client and server on Basic Auth*

On the server side, there needs to be some code to decode the authentication string and load the user data from the session storage used (normally a database).

Aside from the fact that this approach is one of the many that will break the nonstateless constraint, it's easy and fast to implement.

▒ **Note** When using this method, if the password for a logged in user is reset, then the login data sent on the request becomes old and the current session is terminated.

Digest Auth

This method is an improvement over the previous one, in the sense that it adds an extra layer of security by encrypting the login information. The communication with the server works the same way, by sending the same headers back and forth.

With this methodology, upon receiving a request for a protected resource, the server will respond with a WWW-Authenticate header and some specific parameters. Here are some of the most interesting:

- *Nounce*: A uniquely generated string. This string needs to be unique on every 401 response.
- *Opaque*: A string returned by the server that has to be sent back by the client unaltered.
- *Qop*: Even though optional, this parameter should be sent to specify the quality of protection needed (more than one token can be sent in this value). Sending `auth` back would imply a simple authentication, whereas sending `auth-int` implies authentication with integrity check.
- *Algorithm*: This string specifies the algorithm used to calculate the checksum response form the client. If not present, then MD5 should be assumed.

For the full list of parameters and implementation details, please refer to the RFC.[16] Here is a list of some of the most interesting ones:

- *Username*: The unencrypted username.
- *URI*: The URI you're trying to access.
- *Response*: The encrypted portion of the response. This proves that you are who you say you are.
- *Qop*: If present, it should be one of the supported values sent by the server.

To calculate the response, the following logic needs to be applied:

```
MD5(HA1:STRING:HA2)
```

Those values for HA1 are calculated as follows:

- If no algorithm is specified on the response, then `MD5(username:realm:password)` should be used.
- If the algorithm is MD5-less, then it should be `MD5(MD5(username:realm:password):nonce:cnonce)`

Those values for HA2 are calculated as follows:

- If qop is `auth`, then `MD5(method:digestURI)` should be used.
- If qop is `auth-int`, then `MD5(method:digestURI:MD5(entityBody))`

Finally, the response will be as follows:

```
MD5(HA1:nonce:nonceCount:clientNonce:HA2) //for the case when "qop" is "auth" or "auth-int"
MD5(HA1:nonce:HA2) //when "qop" is unspecified.
```

[16] See `https://www.ietf.org/rfc/rfc2617.txt`.

The main issue with this method is that the encryption used is based on MD5, and in 2004 it was proven that this algorithm is not collision resistant, which basically means a man-in-the-middle attack would make it possible for an attacker to get the necessary information and generate a set of valid credentials.

A possible improvement over this method, just like with its "Basic" brother, would be adding TSL; this would definitely help make it more secure.

OAuth 1.0a

OAuth 1.0a is the most secure of the four nonstateless methodologies described in this section. The process is a bit more tedious than the ones described earlier (see Figure 2-8), but the trade-off here is a significantly increased level of security.

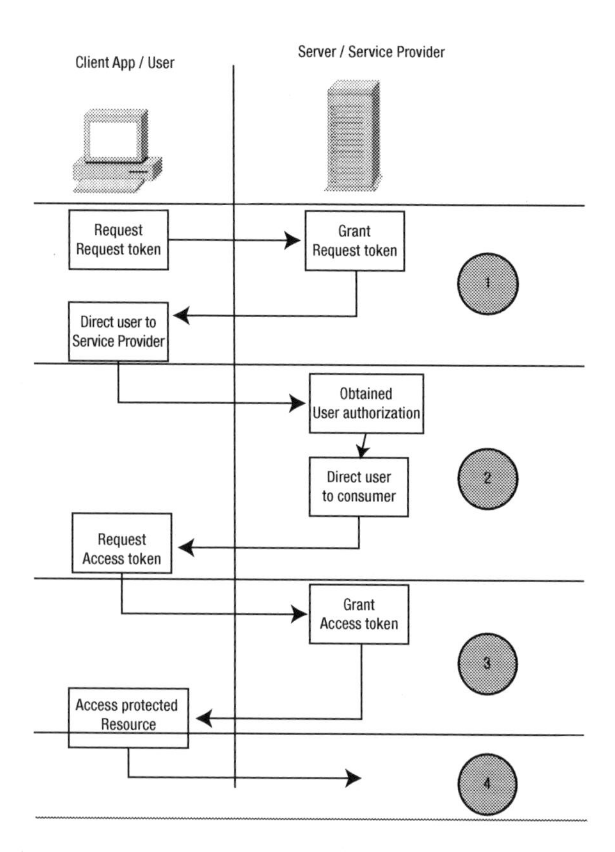

Figure 2-8. *The interaction between client and server*

In this case, the service provider has to allow the developer of the client app to register the app on the provider's web site. By doing so, the developer obtains a consumer key (a unique identifying key for his application) and the consumer secret. Once that process is done, the following steps are required:

- The client app needs a request token. The purpose is to receive the user's approval and then request an access token. To get the request token, a specific URL must be provided by the server; in this step, the consumer key and the consumer secret are used.

- Once the request token is obtained, the client must make a request using the token on a specific server URL (i.e., `http://provider.com/oauth/authorize`) to get authorization from the end user.
- After authorization from the user is given, then the client app makes a request to the provider for an access token and a token secret key.
- Once the access token and secret token are obtained, the client app is able to request protected resources for the provider on behalf of the user by signing each request.

For more details on how this method works, please refer to the complete documentation.[17]

OAuth 2.0

OAuth 2.0 is meant to be the evolution of OAuth 1.0a; it focuses on client developer simplicity. The main problem with implementations of systems that worked with OAuth 1.0 was the complexity implied in the last step: signing every request.

Due to its complexity, the last step is the key weak point of the algorithm: if either the client or server makes a tiny mistake, then the requests will not validate. Even when the same aspect made it the only methodology that didn't need to work on top of SSL (or TSL), this benefit wasn't enough.

OAuth 2.0 tries to simplify the last step by making some key changes, mainly:

- It relies on SSL (or TSL) to ensure that the information sent back and forth is encrypted.
- Signatures are not required for requests after the token has been generated.

To summarize, this version of OAuth tries to simplify the complexity introduced by OAuth 1.0, while sacrificing security at the same time (by relying on TSL to ensure data encryption). It is the preferred method over OAuth 1.0 if the devices you're dealing with have support for TSL (computers, mobile devices, etc.); otherwise, you might want to consider using other options.

A Stateless Alternative

As you've seen, the alternatives you have when it comes to implementing a security protocol to allow users to sign into a RESTful API are not stateless, and even though you should be prepared to make that commitment in order to gain the benefits of tried and tested ways of securing your application, there is a fully REST compatible way of doing it as well.

If you go back to Chapter 1, the stateless constraints basically imply that any and all states of the communication between client and server should be included on every request made by the client. This of course includes the user information, so if you want to have stateless authentication, you need to include that in your requests as well.

If you want to ensure the authenticity of each request, you can borrow the signature step of OAuth 1.0a and apply it on every request by using a pre-established secret key between the client and the server, and a MAC (Message Authentication Code) algorithm to do the signing (see Figure 2-9).

---

[17]See `http://oauth.net/core/1.0a/`.

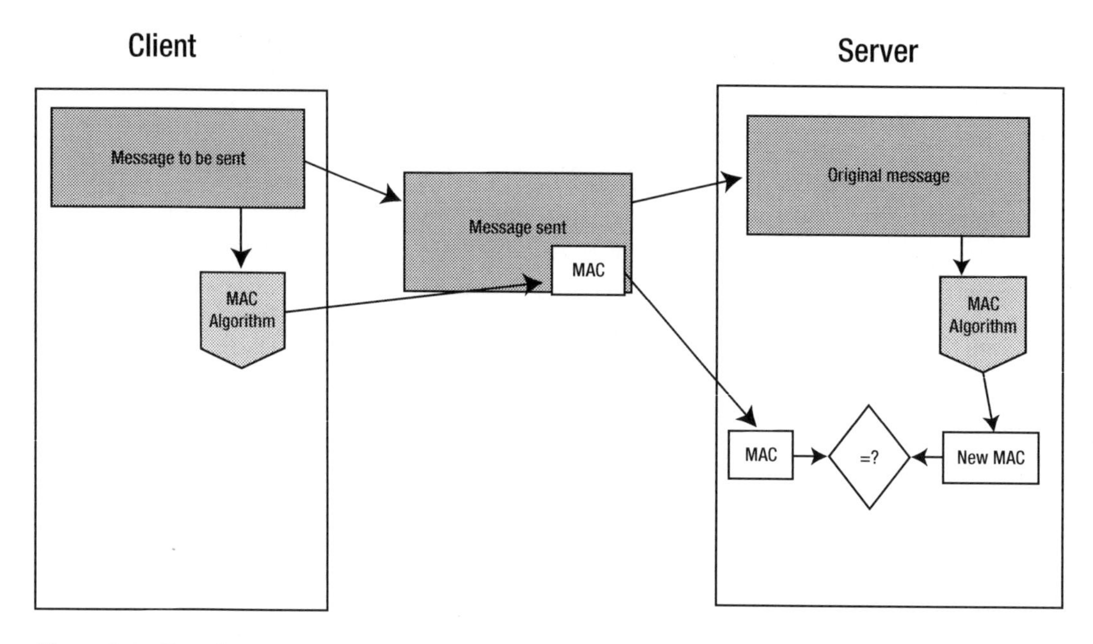

Figure 2-9. *How the MAC signing process works*

As you're keeping it stateless, the information required to generate the MAC needs to also be sent as part of the request, so the server can re-create the result and corroborate its validity.

This approach has some clear advantages in our case, mainly:

- It's simpler than both OAuth 1.0a and OAuth 2.0.
- Zero storage is needed, since any and all required information to validate the encryption needs to be sent on every request.

Scalability

Last but certainly not least is *scalability*.

Scalability is usually an underestimated aspect of API design, mainly because it's quite difficult to fully understand and predict the reach one API will have before it launches. It might be easier to estimate this if the team has previous experience with similar projects (e.g., Google has probably gotten quite good at calculating their scalability for new APIs before launch day), but if it's their first one, then it might not be as easy.

A good API should be able to scale, that means, it should be able to handle as much traffic as it gets without compromising its performance. But it also means it should not spend resources if they're not needed. This is not only a reflection of the hardware that the API resides on (although that is an important aspect) it's also a reflection of the underlying architecture of that API.

Over the years, the classic monolithic design in software architecture has been migrating into a fully distributed one, so splitting the API into different modules that interact with each other makes sense.

This provides the flexibility needed to not only scale up or down the resources that are affected, but to also provide fault tolerance, help developers maintain cleaner code bases amongst other advantages.

The following image (Figure 2-10) shows a standard monolithic design, having your app inside one server, living like one single entity.

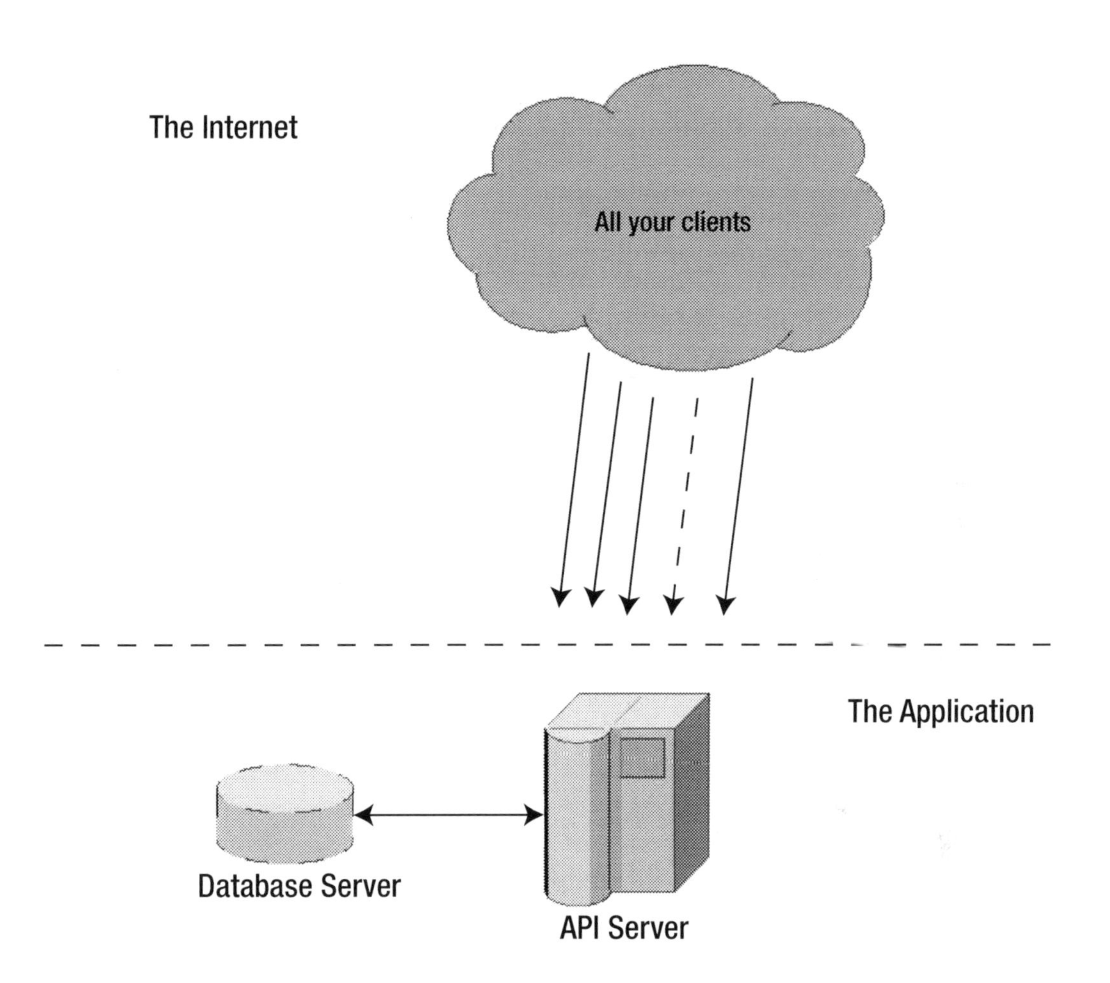

Figure 2-10. *Simple diagram of a monolithic architecture*

In Figure 2-11 you see a distributed design, if compared with the previous one, you can see where the advantages come from (better resource usage, fault tolerance, easier to scale up or down, and so on).

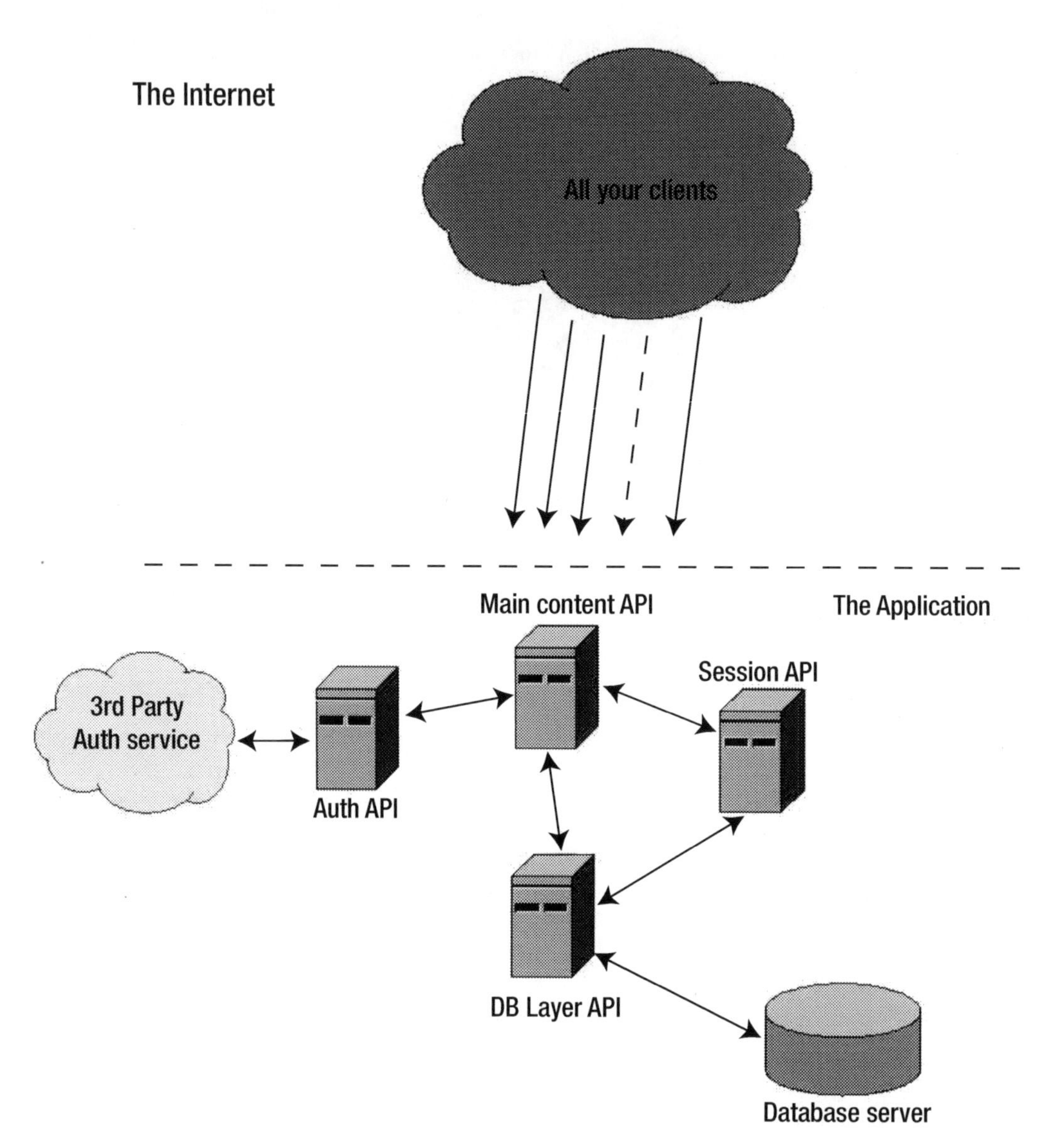

Figure 2-11. *A diagram showing an example of a distributed architecture.*

Achieving a distributed architecture to ensure scalability using REST is quite simple. Fielding's paper proposes a distributed system based on a client-server scheme.

So splitting the entire system into a set of smaller APIs, having them talk to each other when required will ensure the advantages mentioned earlier.

For instance, let's look at an internal system for a bookstore (Table 2-4), the main entities would be:

Table 2-4. *List of Entities and Their Role Inside the System*

Entity	Description
Books	Represents the inventory of the store. It'll control everything from book data, to number of copies, and so forth.
Clients	Contact information of clients.
Users	Internal bookstore users, they will have access to the system.
Purchases	Records information about book sales.

Now, consider that system on a small bookstore, one that is just starting and has just a few employees. It's very tempting to go with a monolithic design, not a lot of resources will be spent and the design is quite simple.

Now, consider what would happen if the small bookstore suddenly grows so much that it expands into several other bookstores, they go from having one store, to 100, employee numbers grow, books need better tracking, purchases sky rocket.

The simple system from before will not be enough to handle such growth. It would require changes to support networking, centralized data storage, distributed access, better storage capacity, and so forth. In other words scaling it up would be too expensive and probably it would require a complete rewrite.

Finally, consider an alternative beginning, what if you took the time to create the first system using a distributed architecture based on REST? Having each sub-system be a different API and having them talk to each other.

Then you would've been able to scale the whole thing much easier, working independently on each sub-system there would be no need for full rewrites and the system could potentially keep growing to meet new needs.

Summary

This chapter covered what the developer community considers a "good API," which means the following:

- Remembering the Developer eXperience (DX).
- Being able to grow and improve without breaking existing clients.
- Having up-to-date documentation.
- Providing correct error handling.
- Providing multiple SDK and libraries.
- Thinking about security.
- Being able to scale, both up and down, as needed.

In the next chapter, you'll learn why Node.js is a perfect match for implementing everything you've learned in this chapter.

CHAPTER 3

Node.js and REST

There are currently too many technologies out there—be it programming languages, platforms, or frameworks. Why is it, then, that Node.js—a project that's hasn't even reached version 1.0 at the time of this writing—is so popular these days?

Advances in hardware make it possible for developers to focus less on hyper-optimizing their code to gain speed, allowing them to focus more on speed of development; thus, a new set of tools has surfaced. These tools make it easier for novice developers to develop new projects, while at the same time provide advanced developers with access to the same type of power they got with the old tools. These tools are the new programming languages and frameworks of today (Ruby on Rails, Laravel, Symfony, Express.js, Node.js, Django, and much more).

In this chapter, I'll go over one of the newest of these: Node.js. It was created in 2009 by Ryan Dahl, and sponsored by Joyent, the company that Dahl worked for. At its core, Node.js[1] utilizes the Google V8[2] engine to execute JavaScript code on the server side. I'll cover its main features to help you understand why it is such a great tool for API development.

The following are some of the aspects of Node.js covered in this chapter:

- *Async programming*: This is a great feature of Node.js. I'll discuss how you can leverage it to gain better results than if using other technologies.
- *Async I/O*: Although related to async programming, this deserves a separate mention because in input/output-heavy applications, this particular feature presents the winning card for choosing Node.js over other technologies.
- *Simplicity*: Node.js makes getting started and writing your first web server very easy. You'll see some examples.
- *Amazing integration with JSON-based services* (like other APIs, MongoDB, etc.).
- *The community and the Node package manager* (npm): I'll go over the benefits of having a huge community of developers using the technology, and how npm has helped.
- *Who's using it?* Finally, I'll quickly go over some of the big companies using Node.js in their production platforms.

[1]See `http://en.wikipedia.org/wiki/Node.js`.
[2]See `http://en.wikipedia.org/wiki/V8_(JavaScript_engine)`.

F. Doglio, *Pro REST API Development with Node.js*, DOI 10.1007/978-1-4842-0917-2_3

Asynchronous Programming

Asynchronous (or async) programming is perhaps at the same time one of the best and most confusing features of Node.js.

Asynchronous programming means that for every asynchronous function that you execute, you can't expect it to return the results before moving forward with the program's flow. Instead, you'll need to provide a callback block/function that will be executed once the asynchronous code finishes.

Figure 3-1 shows a regular, non-asynchronous flow.

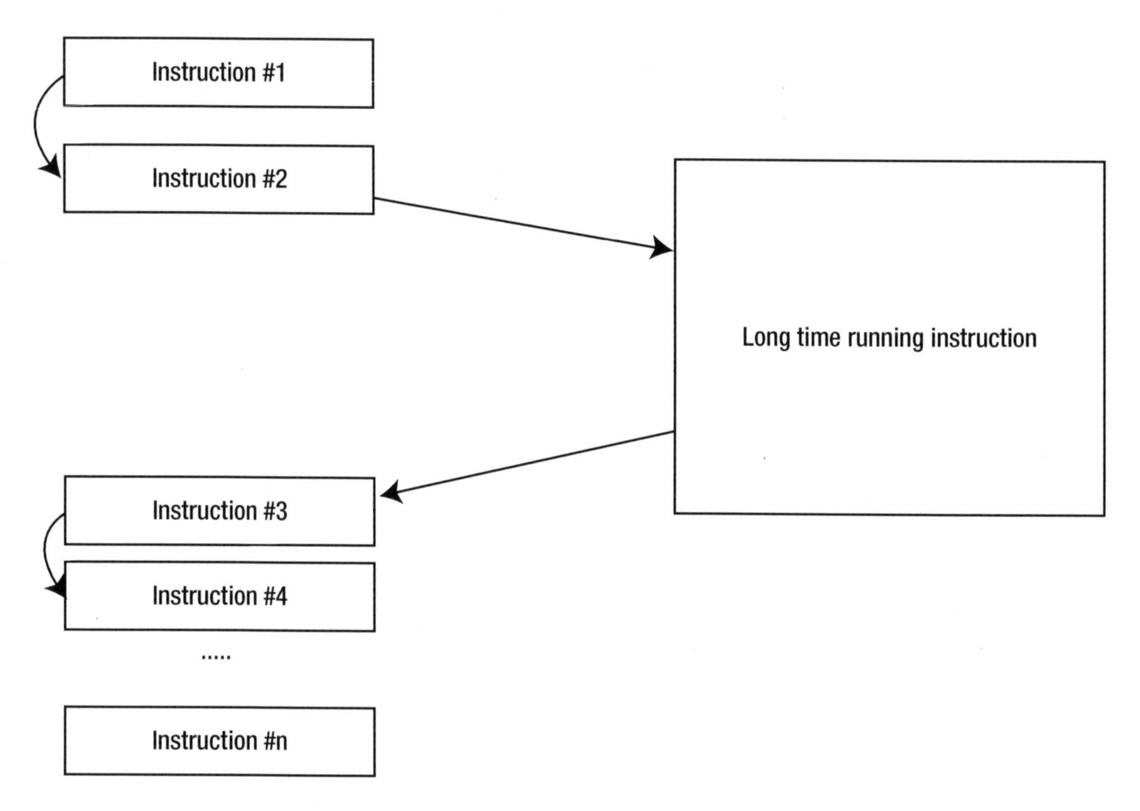

Figure 3-1. *A synchronous execution flow*

Figure 3-1 represents a set of instructions that run in a synchronous manner. In order to execute Instruction #4, you need to wait as long as the "long time running instruction" takes, and then wait for Instruction #3 to finish. But what if Instruction #4 and Instruction #3 weren't really related? What if you didn't really mind in which order Instruction #3 and Instruction #4 executed in relationship to each other?

Then you could make the "long time running instruction" executed in an asynchronous manner and provide Instruction #3 as a callback to that, allowing you to execute Instruction #4 much sooner. Figure 3-2 shows how that would look.

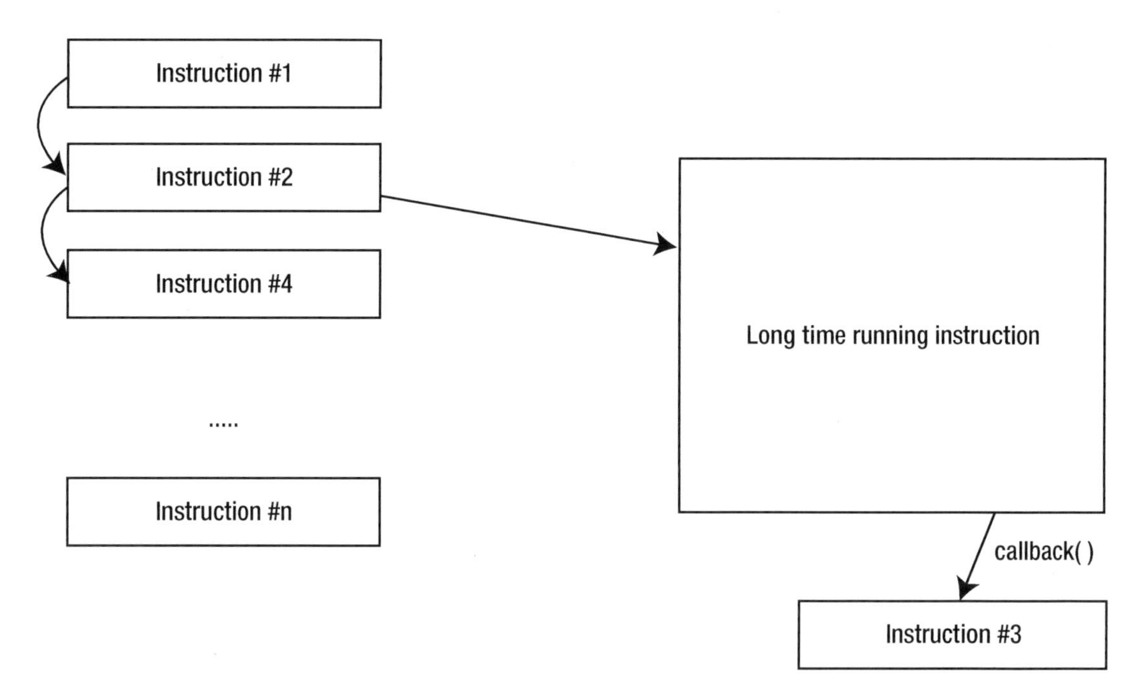

Figure 3-2. *An asynchronous execution flow*

Instead of waiting for it to finish, Instruction #4 is executed right after Instruction #2 starts the asynchronous "long time running instruction".

This is a very simple example of the potential benefits of asynchronous programming. Sadly, like with most in this digital world, nothing comes without a price, and the added benefits also come with a nasty trade-off: debugging asynchronous code can be a real head-breaker.

Developers are trained to think of their code in the sequential way they write it, so debugging a code that is not sequential can be difficult to newcomers.

For instance, Listings 3-1 and 3-2 show the same piece of code written in a synchronous and an asynchronous manner, respectively.

Listing 3-1. Synchronous Version of a Simple Read File Operation

```
console.log("About to read the file...")
var content = Fs.readFileSync("/path/to/file")
console.log("File content: ", content)
```

Listing 3-2. Asynchronous Version of a Simple File Read Operation with a Common Mistake

```
console.log("About to read the file...")
var content = ""
fs.readFile("/path/to/file", function(err, data) {
   content = data
})
console.log("File content: ", content)
```

If you haven't guessed it yet, Listing 3-2 will print the following:

```
File content:
```

And the reason for that is directly related to the diagram shown in Figure 3-3. Let's use it to see what's going on with the buggy asynchronous version.

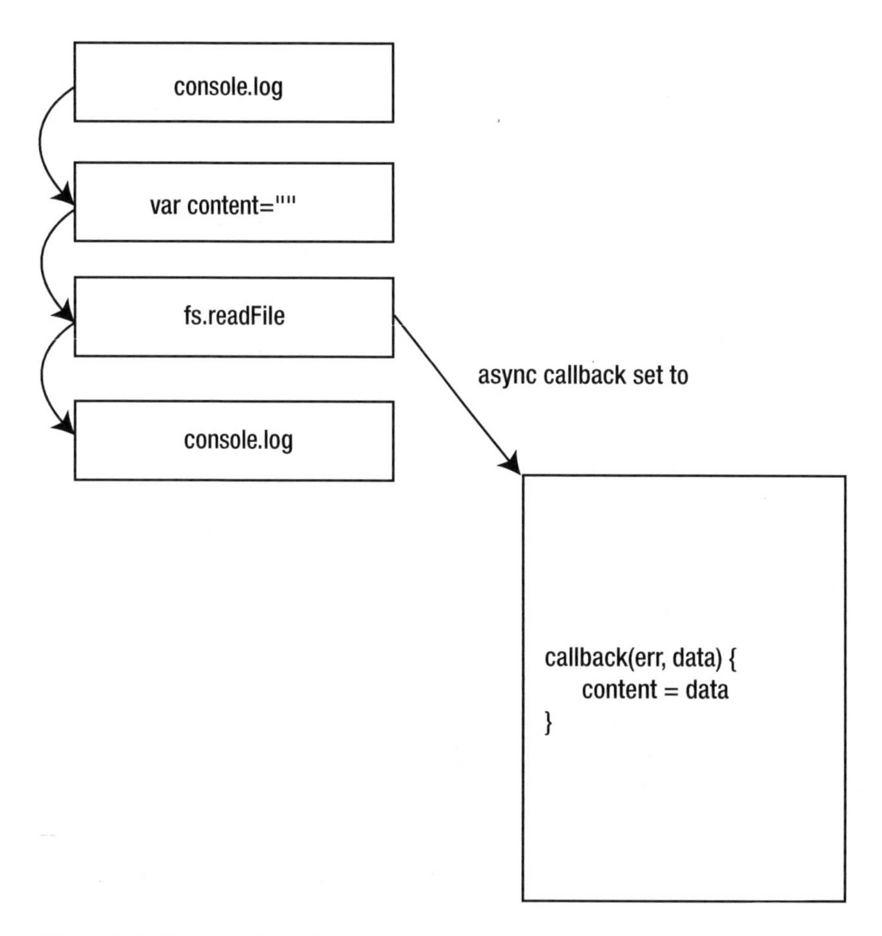

Figure 3-3. *The error from Listing 3-2*

It's pretty clear why the content of the file is not being written: the callback is being executed after the last `console.log` line. This is a very common mistake by new developers, not only with Node.js, but more specifically with AJAX calls on the front end. They set up their code in a way to use the content returned by the asynchronous call before it actually ends.

To finish the example, Listing 3-3 shows how the code needs to be written to properly work.

Listing 3-3. Correct Version of the Asynchronous File Read Operation

```
console.log("About to read the file...")
var content = ""
fs.readFile("/path/to/file", function(err, data) {
   content = data
   console.log("File content: ", content)
})
```

Simple. You just moved the last `console.log` line into the callback function, so you're sure that the `content` variable is set correctly.

Async Advanced

Asynchronous programming is not just about making sure that you set up the callback function correctly, it also allows for some interesting flow control patterns that can be used to improve the efficiency of the app.

Let's look at two distinct and very useful control flow patterns for asynchronous programming: *parallel flow* and *serial flow*.

Parallel Flow

The idea behind parallel flow is that the program can run a set of nonrelated tasks in parallel, but only call the callback function provided (to gather their collective outputs) after all tasks have finished executing.

Basically, Listing 3-4 shows what you want.

Listing 3-4. Signature of the Parallel Function

```
//functionX symbols are references to individual functions
parallel([function1, function2, function3, function4], function(data) {
   ///do something with the combined output once they all finished
})
```

In order to know when each of the functions passed in the array have finished execution, they'll have to execute a callback function with the results of their operation. The callback will be the only attribute they receive. Listing 3-5 shows the parallel function.

Listing 3-5. Implementation of the Parallel Function

```
function parallel(funcs, callback) {
     var results = [],
           callsToCallback = 0
     funcs.forEach(function(fn) { // iterate over all functions
       setTimeout(fn(done), 200) // and call them with a 200 ms delay
      })

    function done(data) { // the functions will call this one when they finish and
they'll pass the results here
        results.push(data)
        if(++callsToCallback == funcs.length) {
           callback(results)
        }
    }
}
```

The implementation in Listing 3-5 is very simple, but it fulfills its task: it runs a set of functions in a parallel way (you'll see that since Node.js runs in a single thread, true parallelism is not possible, so this is as close as you can get).This type of control flow is particularly useful when dealing with calls to external services.

Let's look at a practical example. Assume your API needs to do several operations that, although aren't related to each other, need to happen before the user can see the results. For instance, load the list of books from the database, query an external service to get news about new books out this week, and log the request into a file. If you were to execute all of those tasks in a series (see Listing 3-6), waiting for one to finish before the next one can be run, then the user would most probably suffer a delay on the response because the total time needed for the execution is the sum of all individual times.

But if instead, you can execute all of them in parallel (see Listing 3-7), then the total time is actually equal to the time it takes the slowest task to execute.[3]

Let's look at both cases in Listings 3-6 and 3-7.

Listing 3-6. Example of a Serial Flow (takes longer)

```
//request handling code...
//assume "db" is already initialized and provides an interface to the data base
db.query("books", {limit:1000, page: 1}, function(books) {
  services.bookNews.getThisWeeksNews(function(news) {
     services.logging.logRequest(request, function() { //nothing returned,
but you need to call it so you know the logging finished
        response.render({listOfBooks: books, bookNews: news})
     })
   })
})
```

Listing 3-7. Example of a Parallel Execution Flow

```
//request handling code...
parallel([
  function(callback) { db.query("books", {limit: 1000, page: 1}, callback) }),
  function(callback) { services.bookNews.getThisWeeksNews(callback) }),
  function(callback) { services.logRequest(request, callback) })
 ], function(data) {
     var books = findData('books', data)
     var news = findData('news', data)
     response.render({listOfBooks: books, bookNews: news})
 })
```

Listings 3-6 and 3-7 show how each approach looks. The `findData` function simply looks into the `data` array, and based on the structure of the items, returns the desired one (first parameter). In the implementation of `parallel` it is needed because you can't be sure in which order the functions finished and then sent back their results.

Aside from the clear speed boost that the code gets, it's also easier to read and easier to add new tasks to the parallel flow—just add a new item to the array.

Serial Flow

The serial flow provides the means to easily specify a list of functions that need to be executed in a particular order. This solution doesn't provide a speed boost like parallel flow does, but it does provide the ability to write such code and keep it clean, staying away from what is normally known as *spaghetti code*.

Listing 3-8 shows what you should try to accomplish.

[3]This is a rough approximation, since the time added by the parallel function needs to be taken into account for an exact number.

Listing 3-8. Signature of the Serial Function

```
serial([
 function1, function2, function3
], function(data) {
   //do something with the combined results
})
```

Listing 3-9 shows what you shouldn't do.

Listing 3-9. Example of a Common Case of Nested Callbacks

```
 function1(function(data1) {
    function2(function(data2) {
     function3(function(data3) {
       //do something with all the output
    }
  }
}
```

You can see how the code in Listing 3-9 could get out of hand if the number of functions kept growing. So the serial approach helps keep the code organized and readable.

Let's look at a possible implementation of the serial function in Listing 3-10.

Listing 3-10. Implementation of the Serial Function

```
function serial(functions, done) {
    var fn = functions.shift() //get the first function off the list

    var results = []
    fn(next)

    function next(result) {
        results.push(result) //save the results to be passed into the final callback
once you don't have any more functions to execute.
        var nextFn = functions.shift()
        if (nextFn) nextFn(next)
        else done(results)
    }
}
```

There are more variations to these functions, like using an error parameter to handle errors automatically, or limiting the number of simultaneous functions in the parallel flow.

All in all, asynchronous programming brings a lot of benefits to implementing APIs. Parallel workflow comes in very handy when dealing with external services, which normally any API would deal with; for instance, database access, other APIs, disk I/O, and so forth. And at the same time, the serial workflow is useful when implementing things like Express.js middleware.[4]

For a fully functional and tested library that thrives on asynchronous programming, please check out async.js.[5]

---

[4]See `http://expressjs.com/guide/using-middleware.html`.
[5]See `https://github.com/caolan/async`.

Asynchronous I/O

A specific case of asynchronous programming relates to a very interesting feature provided by Node.js: asynchronous I/O. This feature is highly relevant to the internal architecture of Node.js (see Figure 3-4). As I've said, Node.js doesn't provide multithreading; it actually works with a single thread that runs an event loop.

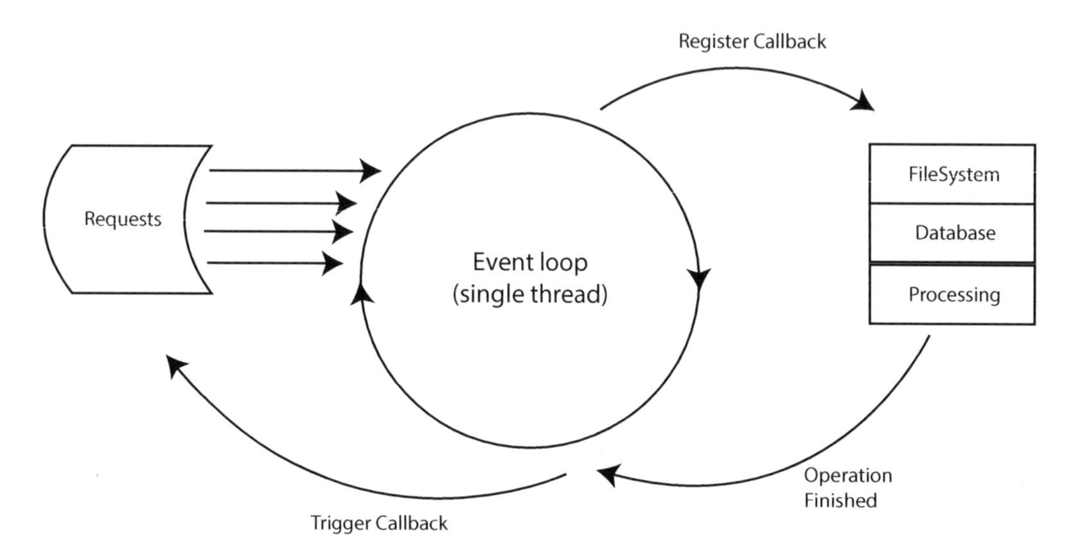

Figure 3-4. *How the EventLoop orchestrates the execution of the code*

In a nutshell, Node.js was designed with the mindset that I/O operations are the actual bottleneck in every operation, not the processing power; so every request received by the node process will work inside the event loop until an I/O operation is found. When that happens, the callback is registered on a separate queue and the main program's flow continues. Once the I/O operation finishes, the callback is triggered and the code inside it is run.

Async I/O vs. Sync I/O

Finally, for the sake of proving that everything I've stated so far is true and that Node.js works best using async I/O, I've done some very simple benchmarking. I've created a simple API with two endpoints:

- `/async`: This reads a 1.6MB file asynchronously before returning a simple JSON response.
- `/sync`: This reads a 1.6MB file synchronously before returning a simple JSON response.

Both endpoints do exactly the same; only in a different manner (see Listing 3-11). The idea is to prove that even in such simple code, the event loop can handle multiple requests better when the underlying code makes use of the asynchronous I/O provided by the platform.

Listing 3-11 is the code of both endpoints; the API was written using Vatican.js.[6]

[6]See `http://www.vaticanjs.info`.

Listing 3-11. Example of Two Endpoints Coded Using the Vatican.js Framework

```
//Async handler
var fs = require("fs")

module.exports = AsyncHdlr;
function AsyncHdlr(_model) { this.model = _model }
//@endpoint (url: /async method: get)
AsyncHdlr.prototype.index = function(req, res, next) {
    fs.readFile(__dirname + "/../file.txt", function (err, content) {
        res.send({
            success: true
        })
    })
}

//Sync handler
var fs = require("fs")

module.exports = SyncHdlr;
function SyncHdlr(_model) { this.model = _model }
//@endpoint (url: /sync method:get)
SyncHdlr.prototype.index = function(req, res, next) {
    var content = fs.readFileSync(__dirname + "/../file.txt")
    res.send({
        success: true
    })
}
```

The benchmark was done using the Apache Benchmark[7] tool, using the following parameters:

- Number of requests: 10,000
- Concurrent requests: 100

The results are shown in Table 3-1.

Table 3-1. *Results from the Benchmark of the Two Endpoints Shown in Listing 3-11*

Synchronous Endpoint	Asynchronous Endpoint
Requests per second: 2411.28 [#/sec.] (mean)	Requests per second: 2960.79 [#/sec.] (mean)
Time per request 41.472 [ms] (mean)	***Time per request: 33.775 [ms] (mean)***
Time per request: 0.415 [ms] (mean, across all concurrent requests)	Time per request: 0.338 [ms] (mean, across all concurrent requests)
Transfer rate: 214.28 [KBps] received	Transfer rate: 263.12 [KBps] received

[7]See http://httpd.apache.org/docs/2.2/programs/ab.html.

As you can see in Table 3-1, for even the simplest of examples, there are 549 more requests being served by the asynchronous code than in the synchronous code in the same amount of time. Another interesting item is that each request is almost 8 milliseconds faster on the asynchronous endpoint; this might not be a huge number, but considering the nonexistent complexity of the code you're using, it's quite relevant.

Simplicity

Node.js (more specifically, JavaScript) is not a complicated language. It follows the basic principles that similar scripting languages follow (like Ruby, Python, and PHP), but with a twist (like all of them do). Node.js is simple enough for any developer to pick up and start coding in no time, and yet it's powerful enough to achieve almost anything developers can set their minds to.

Although JavaScript is an amazing language, and a focus of this book, like I've said and will keep saying: there are no silver bullets when it comes to programming. JavaScript has gained a lot of traction over the years, but it has also gained a lot of haters, and they have their very valid reasons: a nonstandard object-oriented model, weird usage of the `this` keyword, a lack of functionality built into the language (it has a lot of libraries dedicated to implementing basic features that come built-in in other languages), and the list goes on. In the end, every tool needs to be chosen based on its strengths. Node.js is a particularly strong option for developing APIs, as you're about to see.

Node.js adds a certain useful flavor to the language, simplifying a developer's life when trying to develop back-end code. It not only adds the required utilities to work with I/O (which front-end JavaScript doesn't have for obvious security reasons), but it also provides stability for all the different flavors of JavaScript that each web browser supports. One example of this is how easy it is to set up a web server with just a few lines of code. Let's look at that in Listing 3-12.

Listing 3-12. Simple Example of a Web Server Written in Node.js

```
var http = require("http")

http.createServer(function(req, res) { //create the server
        //request handler code here
});

http.listen(3000) //start it up on port 3000
```

JavaScript also has the advantage of being the standard front-end language for all commercial web browsers, which means that if you're a web developer with front-end experience, you have certainly come across JavaScript.

This makes it simpler for the developer who's migrating from the front end into the back end; since the language basics haven't changed, you only need to learn about the new things, and change into a back-end mindset. At the same time, this helps companies find Node.js developers faster.

With all that in mind, let's look at some of the main characteristics of JavaScript that make it such a simple (and yet powerful) option.

Dynamic Typing

Dynamic typing is a basic characteristic, present in most common languages nowadays, but it's not less powerful because of that. This little feature allows the developer to not have to think too much when declaring a variable; just give it a name and move on.

Listing 3-13 shows something you can't do with a statically typed language.

Listing 3-13. Example of Code Taking Advantage Of Dynamic Typing

```
var a, b, tmp //declare the variables (just give them names)

//initialize them with different types
a = 10
b = "hello world"
//now swap the values
tmp = a
a = b //even with automatic casting, a language like C won't be able to cast "hello
world" into an integer value
b = tmp

console.log(a) //prints "hello world"
console.log(b) //prints 10
```

Object-Oriented Programming Simplified

JavaScript it not an object-oriented language, but it does have support for some of these features (see Listing 3-14 and Listing 3-16). You'll have enough of them to conceptualize problems and solutions using objects, which is always a very intuitive way of thinking, but at the same time, you're not dealing with concepts like polymorphism, interfaces, or others that despite helping to structure code, have proven to be dispensable when designing applications.

Listing 3-14. Simplified Object Orientation Example

```
var myObject = { //JS object notation helps simplify definitions
        myAttribute: "some value",
        myMethod: function(param1, param2) {
                //does something here
        }
}
//And the just...
myObject.myMethod(...)
```

Whereas with other languages, like Java (a strongly object-oriented language), you would have to do what's shown in Listing 3-15.

Listing 3-15. Example of a Class Definition in Java

```
class myClass {
        public string myAttribute;
        public void myClass() {
        }
        public void myMethod(int param1, int param2) {
                //does something here
        }
}

//And then
myClass myObj = new myClass();
myObj.myMethod(...);
```

Much less verbose, isn't it?

In Listing 3-16, let's look at another example of the powerful object orientation that you have available.

Listing 3-16. Another Example of the Features Provided by Object Orientation in JavaScript

```
var aDog = { //behave like a dog
        makeNoise: function() {
                console.log("woof!");
        }
}

var aCat = { //behave like a cat
        makeNoise: function() {
                console.log("Meewww!");
        }
}

var myAnimal = { //our main object
        makeNoise: function() {
                console.log("cri... cri....")
        },
        speak: function() {
                this.makeNoise()
        }
}

myAnimal.speak() //no change, so.. crickets!
myAnimal.speak.apply(aDog) //this will print "woof!"
//switch behavior
myAnimal.speak.apply(aCat) //this will now print "Meewww!"
```

You were able to encapsulate a simple behavior into an object and pass it into another object to automatically overwrite its default one. That's something that's built into the language; you didn't have to write any specific code to achieve this feature.

Prototypal Inheritance

Linked to the one above, the *prototypal inheritance* feature allows for incredibly easy extension of your objects at any moment of their life cycle; powerful and simple.

Let's look at Listing 3-17 to understand this better.

Listing 3-17. Example of Prototypal Inheritance in JavaScript

```
var Parent = function() {
        this.parentName = "Parent"
}

var Child = function() {
}

Child.prototype = new Parent()

var childObj = new Child();
console.log(childObj.parentName)
```

```
console.log(childObj.sayThanks) //that's undefined so far

Parent.prototype.sayThanks = function() { //you "teach" the method to the parent
        console.log("Thanks!")
}

console.log(childObj.sayThanks()) //and booom! the child suddenly can say thanks now
```

Did you dynamically affect the parent object—and then the child suddenly updated? Well yes, that just happened! Powerful? I'd say so!

Functional Programming Support

JavaScript is not a functional programming language; but then again, it does have support for some of its features (see Listings 3-18, 3-19, and 3-20), such as having first-class citizen functions , allowing you to pass them around like parameters, and return closures easily. This feature makes it possible to work with callbacks, which, as you've already seen, is the basis for asynchronous programming.

Let's look at a quick and simple functional programming example in Listing 3-18 (remember, JavaScript provides only some functional programming goodies, not all of them). Create an adder function.

Listing 3-18. Simple Example of an Adder Function Defined Using Functional Programming

```
function adder(x) {
  return function(y) {
    return x+y
  }
}

var add10 = adder(10) //you create a new function that adds 10 to whatever you pass to it.
console.log(add10(100)) //will output 110
```

Let's look at a more complex example, an implementation of the map function, which allows you to transform the values of an array by passing the array and the transformation function. Let's first look at how you'd use the *map* function.

Listing 3-19. Example of a Map Function Being Used

```
map([1,2,3,4], function(x) { return x * 2 }) //will return [2,4,6, 8]
map(["h","e","l","l","o"], String.prototype.toUpperCase) //will return ["H","E","L","L","O"]
```

Now let's look at a possible implementation using the functional approach.

Listing 3-20. Implementation of a Map Function, Like the One Used in Listing 3-19

```
function reduce(list, fn, init) {
        if(list.length == 0) return init
        var value = list[0]
        init.push(fn.apply(value, [value])) //this will allow us to get both the
functions that receive the value as parameters and the methods that use it from it's
context (like toUpperCase)
        return reduce(list.slice(1), fn, init) //iterate over the list using it's tail
(everything but the first element)
}
```

```
function map(list, fn) {
	return reduce(list, fn, [])
}
```

Duck Typing

Have you ever heard the phrase "If it looks like a duck, swims like a duck, and quacks like a duck, it probably is a duck."? Well then, it's the same for typing in JavaScript. The type of a variable is determined by its content and properties, not by a fixed value. So the same variable can change its type during the life cycle of your script. Duck typing is both a very powerful feature and a dangerous feature at the same time.

Listing 3-21 offers a simple demonstration.

Listing 3-21. Quick Example of Duck Typing in JavaScript

```
var foo = "bar"
console.log(typeof foo) //will output "string"
foo = 10
console.log(typeof foo) //this will now output "number"
```

Native Support for JSON

This is a tricky one, since JSON actually spawned from JavaScript, but let's not get into the whole chicken-and-egg thing here. Having *native* support for the main transport language used nowadays is a big plus.

Listing 3-22 is a simple example following the JSON syntax.

Listing 3-22. Example of How JSON Is Natively Supported by JavaScript

```
var myJSONProfile = {
	"first_name": "Fernando",
	"last_name": "Doglio",
	"current_age": 30,
	"married": true,
	"phone_numbers": [
		{
			"home_phone": "59881000293",
			"cell_phone": "59823142242"
		}
	]
}

//And you can interact with that JSON without having to parse it or anything
console.log(myJSONProfile.first_name, myJSONProfile.last_name)
```

This particular feature is especially useful in several cases; for instance, when working with a document-based storage solution (like MongoDB) because the modeling of data ends up being native in both places (your app and the database). Also, when developing an API, you've already seen that the transport language of choice these days is JSON, so the ability to format your responses directly with native notation (you could even just output your entities, for that matter) is a very big plus when it comes to ease of use.

The list could be extended, but those are some pretty powerful features that JavaScript and Node.js bring to the table without asking too much of the developer. They are quite easy to understand and use.

▒ **Note** The features mentioned are not unique to JavaScript; other scripting languages have some of them as well.

---

npm: The Node Package Manager

Another point in favor of Node.js is its amazing package manager. As you might know by now (or are about to find out), development in Node is very module dependent, meaning that you're not going to be developing the entire thing; most likely you'll be reusing someone else's code in the form of modules.

This is a very important aspect of Node.js, because this approach allows you to focus on what makes your application unique, and lets the generic code be integrated seamlessly. You don't have to recode the library for HTTP connectivity, or your route handler on every project (in other words, you don't have to keep reinventing the wheel); just set the dependencies of your project into the `package.json` file, using the best-suited module names, and then npm will take care of going through the whole dependency tree and install everything needed (think of APT for Ubuntu or Homebrew for Mac).

The amount of active users and modules available (more than 100,000 packages and more than 600 million downloads a month) assures you that you'll find what you need; and in the rare occasions when you don't, you can contribute by uploading that specific module to the registry and help the next developer that comes looking for it.

This amount of modules can also be a bad thing since such a large number means that there will be several modules that try to do the same thing. (For instance, email-validation, sane-email-validation, mailcover, and mailgun-email-validation, all try to do the same thing—validate an email address using different techniques; depending on your needs, you have to pick one.) You have to browse through them to find the best suited candidate.

This is all possible thanks to the amazing community of developers that formed since Node.js hit the shelves in 2009.

To start using npm, just visit their site at `www.npmjs.org`. There you'll see a list of recently updated packages to get you started, and some of the most popular ones as well.

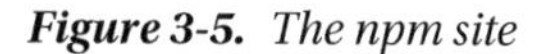

Figure 3-5. *The npm site*

If want to install it directly, just write the following line into your Linux console:

```
$ curl https://www.npmjs.org/install.sh | sh
```

You need to have Node.js version 0.8+ installed to use it properly. Once that is done, you can begin installing modules by simply typing:

```
$ npm install [MODULE_NAME]
```

This command downloads the specified module into a local folder called `node_modules`; so try to run it from within your project's folder.

You can also use npm to develop your own modules and publish them into the site by using the following:

```
$ npm publish #run this command from within your project's folder
```

The preceding command takes attributes from the `package.json` file, package the module, and upload everything into npm's registry. After that, you can go into the site and check for your package; it'll be listed there.

▒ **Note** Aside from checking out `www.npmjs.org`, you can also check the Google Groups nodejs[8] and nodejs-dev[9] for a direct connection to people in the Node.js community.

Who's Using Node.js?

This entire book is meant to validate and provide examples of how good Node.js is when it comes to developing RESTful systems, but also, how valid the idea of having Node.js powered systems running in production (this is the hardest obstacle to overcome, especially when trying to convince your boss of switching stacks into a Node.js based one).

But what better validation then, that to look at some of the most important users of Node.js in production?

- *PayPal*: Uses Node.js to power its web application.
- *eBay*: Uses Node.js mainly due to the benefits that asynchronous I/O brings.
- *LinkedIn*: The entire back-end mobile stack is done in Node.js. The two reasons for using it are scale and performance gained over the previous stack.
- *Netflix*: Uses Node.js on several services. Often writes about experiences using Node.js on its tech blog at `http://techblog.netflix.com`.
- *Yahoo!*: Uses Node.js on several products, such as Flickr, My Yahoo!, and home page).

This list could go on and include a very large list of other companies, some more well-known than others, but the point remains: Node.js is used for production services all over the Internet, and it handles all kinds of traffic.

Summary

This chapter covered the advantages of Node.js for the common developer, especially how its features improve the performance of I/O-heavy systems such as APIs.

In the next chapter, you'll get more hands-on and learn about the basic architecture and tools you'll use to develop the API in the final chapter.

---

[8]See `https://groups.google.com/forum/#!forum/nodejs`.
[9]See `https://groups.google.com/forum/#!forum/nodejs-dev`.

CHAPTER 4

Architecting a REST API

It is extremely important to understand a REST-based architecture, meaning how the system will look if you're basing all of your services in the REST style. But it is equally important to know what the internal architecture of those REST services will look like before you start working.

In Node.js there are several modules out there, with thousands of daily downloads that can help you create an API without having to worry too much about the internal aspects of it. And that might be a good idea if you're in a hurry to get the product out, but since you're here to learn, I'll go over all the components that make up a standard, general-purpose REST API.

The modules are mentioned, but I won't go into details on how they're used or anything; that will come in the next chapter— so keep reading!

For the purpose of this book, I'll take the traditional approach when it comes to architecting the API, and you'll use an MVC pattern (model-view-controller); although you might be familiar with other options, it is one of the most common ones and it normally fits well as a web use case.

The basic internal architecture of a RESTful API contains the following items:

- *A request handler*. This is the focal point that receives every request and processes it before doing anything else.
- *A middleware/pre-process chain*. These guys help shape the request and provide some help for authentication control.
- *A routes handler*. After the request handler is done, and the request itself has been checked and enriched with everything you need, this component figures out who needs to take care of the request.
- *The controller*. This guy is responsible for all requests done related to one specific resource.
- *The Model*. Also known as the *resource* in our case. You'll focus most of the logic related to the resource in here.
- *The representation layer*. This layer takes care of creating the representation that is visible to the client app.
- *The response handler*. Last but certainly not least, the response handler takes care of sending the representation of the response back to the client.

Note As I've stated several times before, this book focuses on HTTP-based REST, which means that any request mentioned in this chapter is an HTTP request, unless otherwise stated.

F. Doglio, *Pro REST API Development with Node.js*, DOI 10.1007/978-1-4842-0917-2_4

The Request Handler, the Pre-Process Chain, and the Routes Handler

The *request handler*, the *pre-process chain*, and the *routes handler* are the first three components in any request to your system, so they're key to having a responsive and fast API. Luckily, you're using Node.js, and as you saw in Chapter 3, Node.js is great at handling many concurrent requests because of its event loop and async I/O.

That being said, let's list the attributes our request handler needs to have for our RESTful system to work as expected:

- It has to gather all the HTTP headers and the body of the request, parse them, and provide a request object with that information.
- It needs to be able to communicate with both the pre-processing chain module and the routes handler in order to figure out which controller needs to be executed.
- It needs to create a response object capable of finishing and (optionally) writing a response back to the client.

Figure 4-1 shows the steps that are part of the initial contact between client and server:

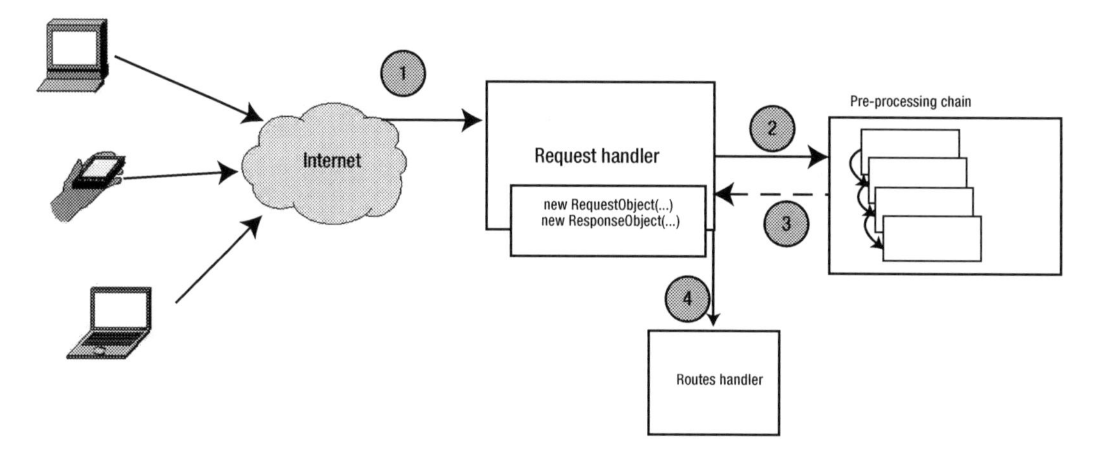

Figure 4-1. *Example of how the request handler and its interactions with other components look*

1. The client application issues a request for a particular resource.
2. The request handler gathers all information. It creates a request object and passes it along to the pre-processing chain.
3. Once finished, the pre-processing chain returns the request object—with whatever changes made to it—to the request handler.
4. Finally, the RH sends the request and response objects to the routes handler so that the process can continue.

There is one problem in Figure 4-1 that jumps right out at you (or it should): if the pre-processing chain takes too long, the request handler must wait for it to finish before handing over the request to the routes handler, and any other incoming request is forced to wait as well.

This can be especially harmful to the performance of the API if the pre-processing chain is doing some heavy-duty tasks, like loading user-related data or querying external services.

Thanks to the fact that you're using Node.js as the basis for everything here, you can easily change the pre-processing chain to be an asynchronous operation. By doing that, the request handler is able to receive new requests while still waiting for the processing chain from the previous request. Figure 4-2 shows how the diagram would change.

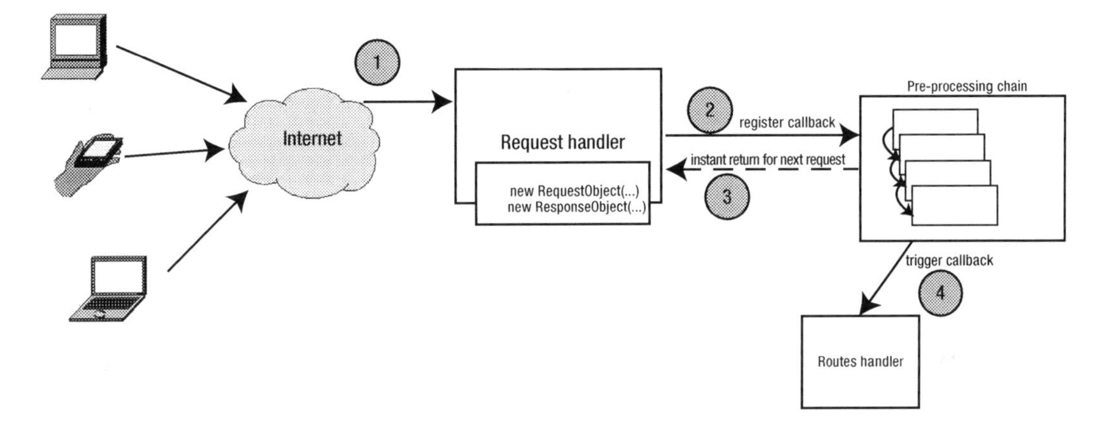

Figure 4-2. *Changes to the architecture show how to improve it by using a callback*

As you can see in Figure 4-2, the change is minimal, at least at the architectural level. The request handler sets up a callback to the routes handler; and that callback is executed once the pre-processing chain is finished. And right after setting up the callback, the request handler is free again for the next request. This clearly provides more freedom to this component, allowing the entire system to process more requests per second.

▒ **Note** This change will not actually speed up the pre-processing chain time of execution, neither will it speed up the time it takes a single request to be finished, but it will allow the API to handle more requests per second, which in practice means avoiding an obvious bottleneck.

As for the pre-processing chain, you'll use it for generic operations, things that are required in most of the routes you'll handle. That way you can extract that code from the handlers and centralize it into small units of code (functions) that are called in sequence for every request.

Most of the modules you'll see in the next chapter have one version of the pre-processing chain. For instance, Express.js calls the functions that can be executed in the chain "middleware." Vatican.js calls them "pre-processors" to differentiate them from the post-processors that the module also provides.

▒ **Tip** The main rule to remember when adding a new function into this chain is that as a good practice, the function should take care of one task, and one task only. (This is generally a good practice to follow on every aspect of software development, some call it the Unix Philosophy, others call it KISS; call it whatever you want, it's a good idea to keep in mind.) That way, it becomes mind-blowingly easy to enable and disable them when testing, even to alter their order. On the other hand, if you start adding functions that take care of more than one thing, like authenticating the user and loading his/her preferences, you'll have to edit the function's code to disable one of those services.

Since you'll want the entire pre-processing to be done asynchronously to release the request handler from waiting for the chain to be done, the chain will use asynchronous serial flow. This way you can be sure of the order of execution; but at the same time, you're free to have these functions perform actions that take longer than normal, like asynchronous calls to external services, I/O operations, and the like.

Let's take a final look at the last diagram. So far it looks great: you're able to handle requests asynchronously and you can do some interesting things to the request by pre-processing it before giving it to the routes handler. But there is one catch: the pre-processing chain is the same for all routes.

That might not be a problem if the API is small enough, but just to be on the safe side, and to provide a fully scalable architecture, let's take a look at another change that can be done over the current version to provide the freedom you require (see Figure 4-3).

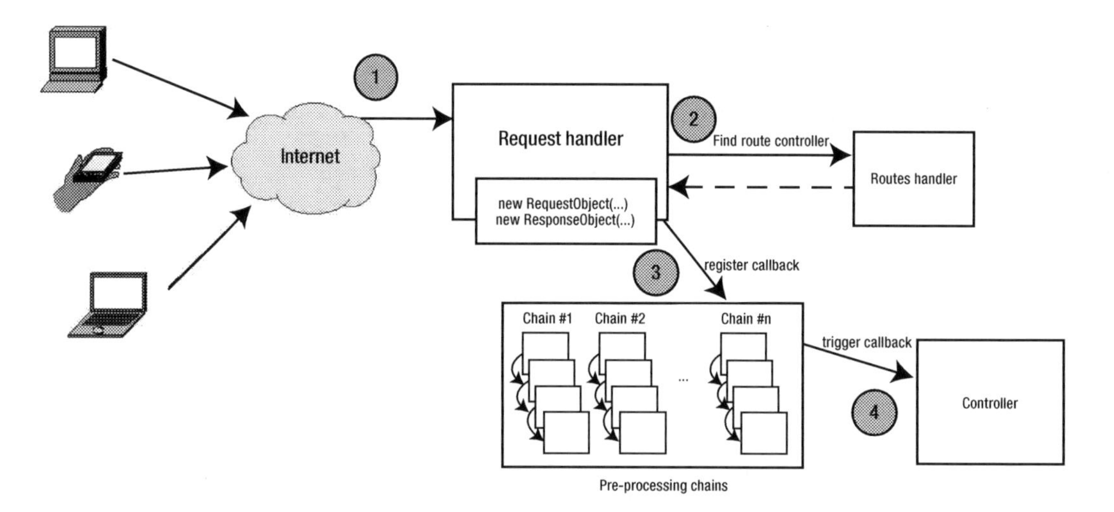

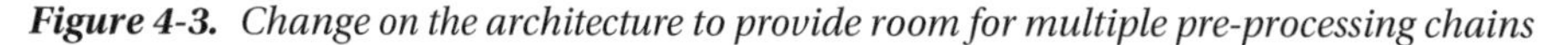

Figure 4-3. *Change on the architecture to provide room for multiple pre-processing chains*

This chain (as shown in Figure 4-3) is bigger than the previous one, but it does solve the scaling problem. The process has now changed into the following steps:

1. The client application issues a request for a particular resource.
2. The request handler gathers all information. It creates a request object and passes it along to the request handler to return the right controller. This action is simple enough to do synchronously. Ideally, it should be done in constant time (O(1)).

3. Once it has the controller, it registers an asynchronous operation with the correct pre-processing chain. This time around, the developer is able to set up as many chains as needed and associates them to one specific route. The request handler also sets up the controller's method to be executed as the callback to the chain's process.

4. Finally, the callback is triggered, and the request object, with the response object passed into the controller's method to continue the execution.

▒ **Note** Step 2 mentions that the controller lookup based on the request should be done in constant time. This is not a hard requirement, but should be the desirable result; otherwise, when handling many concurrent requests, this step might become a bottleneck that can affect subsequent requests.

MVC: a.k.a. Model–View–Controller

The model-view- controller (MVC) architectural pattern[1] is probably *the most well-known pattern out there*. Forget about the Gang of Four's design patterns,[2] forget about everything you learned about software design and architectural patterns; if you're comfortable with MVC, you have nothing to worry about.

Actually, that's not true; well, most of it isn't anyway. MVC *is* currently among the most well-known and used design patterns on web projects (that much is true). That being said, you should not forget about the others; in fact, I highly recommend you actually get familiar with the most common ones (aside from MVC of course), like Singleton, Factory, Builder, Adapter, Composite, Decorator, and so forth. Just look them up, and read and study some examples; it's always handy to have them as part of your tool box.

Going back to MVC, even though it has become really popular in the last few years, especially since 2007 (coincidently the year when version 2 of Ruby on Rails , a popular web framework that had MVC as part of its core architecture, was released), this bad boy is not new. In fact, it was originally described by Krasner and Pope in 1988 at SmallTalk-80[3] as a design pattern for creating user interfaces.

The reason why it is such a popular pattern on web projects is because it fits perfectly into the multilayer architecture that the web provides. Think about it: due to the client-server architecture, you already have two layers there, and if you organized code to split some responsibilities between orchestration and business logic, you gain one more layer on the server side, which could translate into the scenario shown in Table 4-1.

Table 4-1. *List of Layers*

Layer	Description
Business logic	You can encapsulate the business logic of the system into different components, which you can call *models*. They represent the different resources that the system handles.
Orchestration	The models know how to do their job, but not when or what kind of data to use. The controllers take care of this.
Representation layer	Handles creating the visual representation of the information. In a normal web application, this is the HTML page. In a RESTful API, this layer takes care of the different representations each resource has.

---

[1]See `http://en.wikipedia.org/wiki/Model%E2%80%93view%E2%80%93controller`.
[2]See `http://www.amazon.com/Design-Patterns-Elements-Reusable-Object-Oriented/dp/0201633612/`.
[3]See `http://dl.acm.org/citation.cfm?id=50757.50759`.

■ **Note** Prior to Table 4-1, I mentioned that the client-server architecture provided the first two layers for MVC, meaning that the client would act as the presentation layer. This is not entirely true, as you see later on, but it does serve as a conceptual layer, meaning that you'll need a way for the application to present the information to the user (client).

Let's look at the diagram in Figure 4-4, which represents Table 4-1.

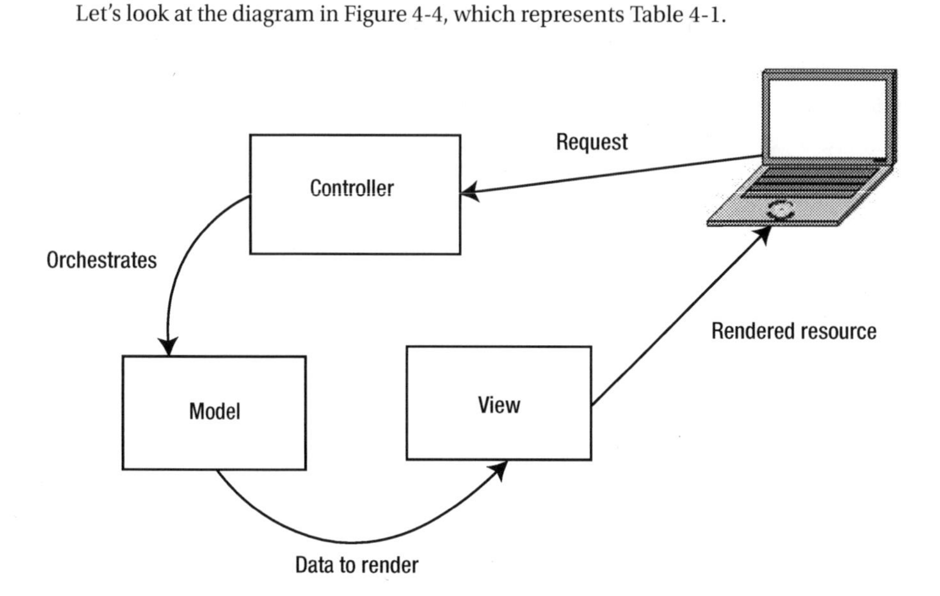

Figure 4-4. *The interaction between the three layers*

Figure 4-4 shows the decoupling of the three components: the controller, the model (which in this case you can also call the resource), and the view. This decoupling allows for a clear definition of each component's responsibilities, which in turn helps keep the code clean and easy to understand.

Although this is great, the pattern has changed a bit ever since it was adopted by some web development frameworks, like Ruby on Rails; it now looks more like what's shown in Figure 4-5.

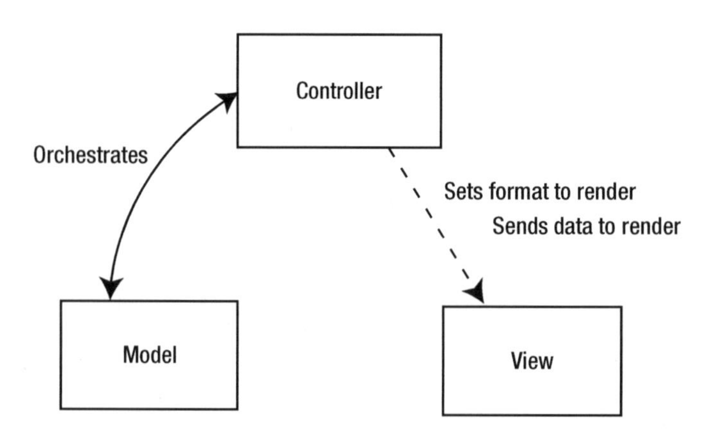

Figure 4-5. *MVC applied to the web*

The current iteration of the pattern removed the relationship between the model and the view, and instead gave the controller that responsibility. The controller now also orchestrates the view.

This final version is the one you'll add into our current growing architecture. Let's take a look at how it will look (see Figure 4-6).

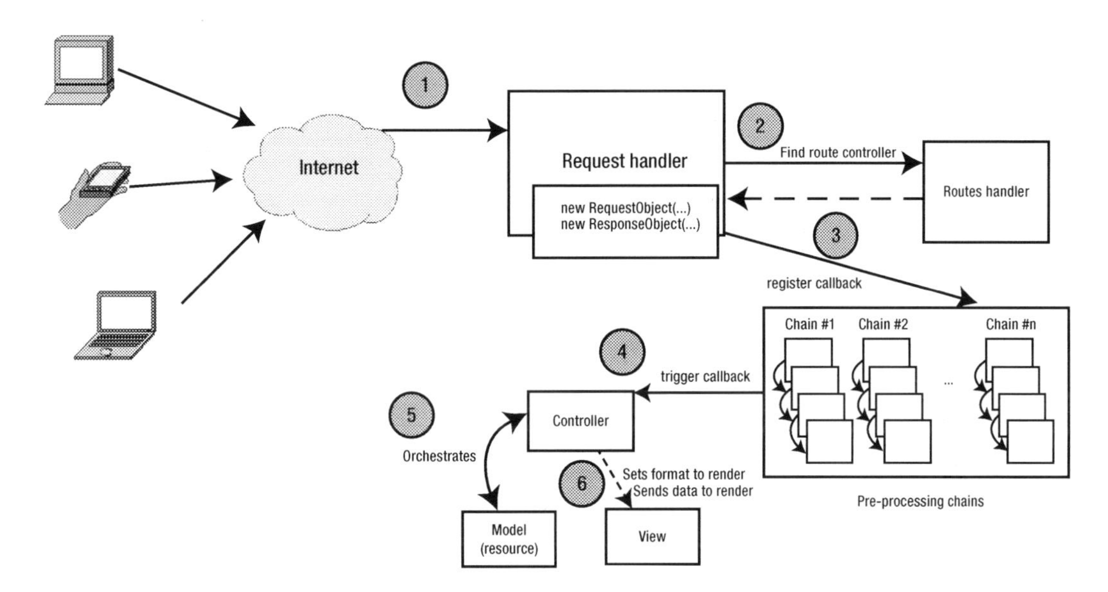

Figure 4-6. *The architecture with the added MVC pattern*

Steps 5 and 6 have been added to our architecture. When the right method on the controller is triggered (in step 4), it handles interacting with the model, gathers the required data, and then sends it over to the view to render it back to the client application.

This architecture works great, but there is still one improvement that can be done. With our RESTful API, the representations are strictly related to the resources data structure, and you can generalize the view into a view layer, which will take care of transforming the resources into whatever format you require. This change simplifies the development since you centralize the entire view-related code into one single component (the view layer).

The diagram in Figure 4-7 might not have changed a lot, but the change in the view box into a view layer represents the generalization of that code, which initially implied that there would be one specific view code for every resource.

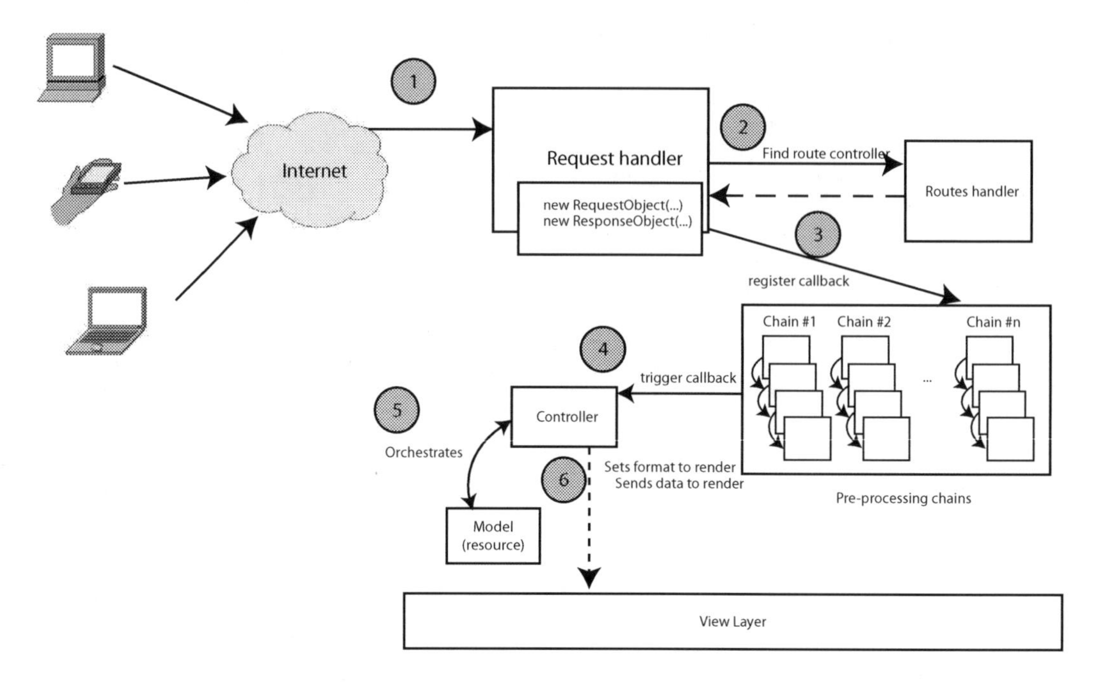

Figure 4-7. *View layer added to the architecture*

Alternatives to MVC

MVC is a great architecture. Nearly every developer is using it or has used it for a web project. Of course, not everyone loves it, because it has suffered the same fate other popular things in the development community have suffered (Ruby on Rails anyone?). If it becomes popular on the Internet, everyone is using it for everything—until they realize that not every project looks like an MVC nail, so you have to start looking at other shapes of hammers (other alternatives architectures).

But luckily, there are alternatives; there are similar architectural patterns that may better suit your needs, depending on the particular aspects of your project. Some of them are direct derivatives of MVC, and others try to approach the same problem from a slightly different angle (I say "slightly" because, as you're about to see, there are things in common).

Hierarchical MVC

Hierarchical MVC[4] is a more complex version of MVC in the sense that you can nest one MVC component inside another one. This gives developers the ability to have things like an MVC group for a page, another MVC group for the navigation inside the page, and a final MVC component for the contents of the page.

This approach is especially helpful when developing reusable widgets that can be plugged into components, since each MVC group is self-contained. It is useful in cases when the data to be displayed comes from different related sources. In these cases, having a HMVC structure helps keep the separation of concerns intact, and avoids coupling between components that shouldn't be.

[4]See `http://en.wikipedia.org/wiki/Hierarchical_model%E2%80%93view%E2%80%93controller`.

Let's look at a very basic example. Think of a user reading a blog post and the related comments underneath it. There are two ways to go about it: with MVC or with HMVC.

With MVC, the request is done to the BlogPosts controller, since that is the main resource being requested; afterward, that controller loads the proper blog post model and using that model's ID, it loads the related comments models. Right there, there is an unwanted coupling between the BlogPosts controller and the comments model. You can see this in the diagram in Figure 4-8.

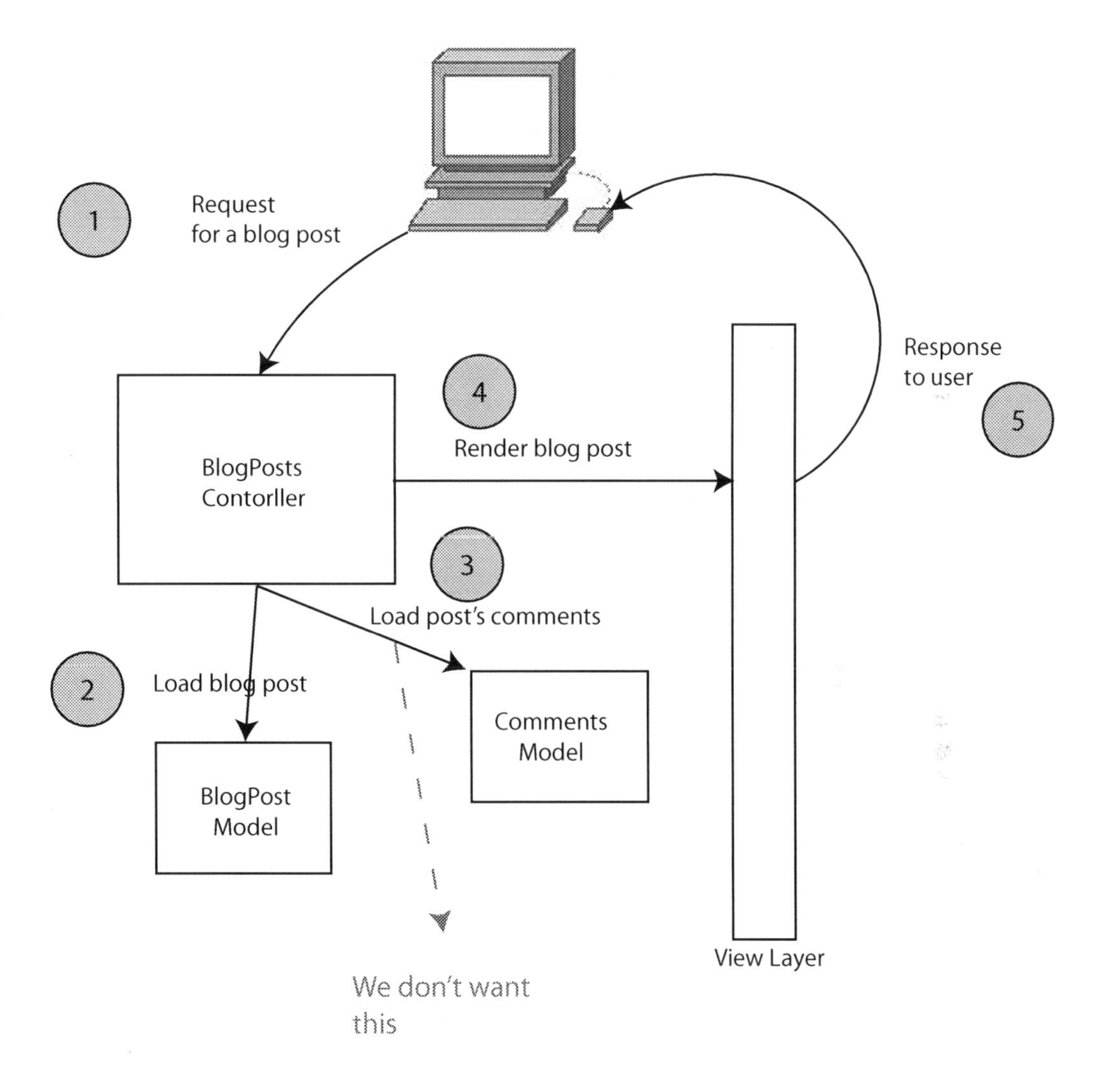

Figure 4-8. *The problem that HMVC tries to solve*

Figure 4-8 shows the coupling that you need to get rid of; it is clearly something that can be improved from an architectural point of view. So let's look at what this would look like using HMVC (see Figure 4-9).

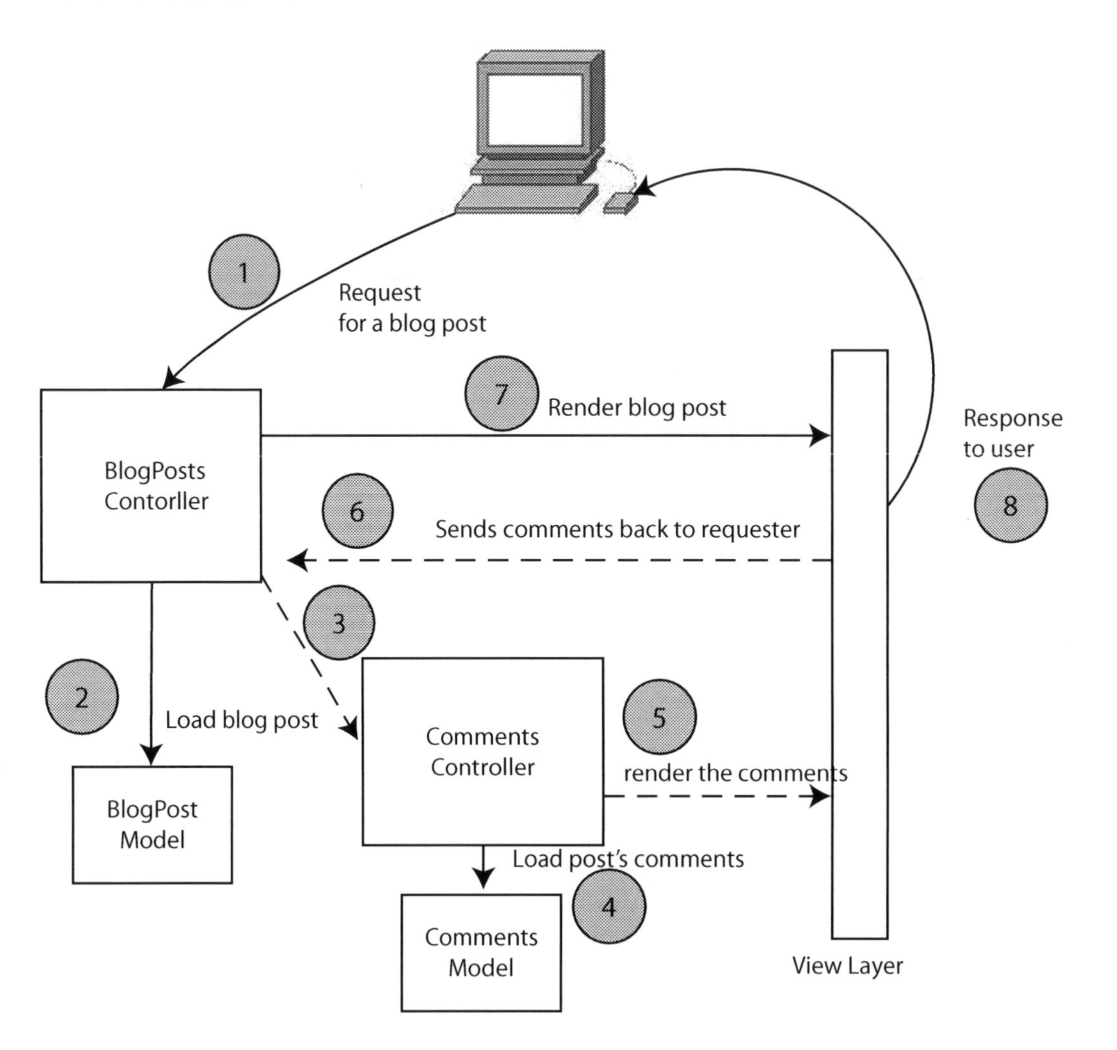

Figure 4-9. *The same diagram with the HMVC pattern applied*

The architecture certainly looks more complex and there are more steps, but it is also cleaner and easier to extend. Now in step 3, you're sending a request to an entirely new MVC component, one in charge of dealing with comments. That component will in turn interact with the corresponding model and with the generic view layer to return the representation of the comments. The representation is received by the BlogPost controller, which attaches it to the data obtained from the BlogPost model and sends everything back into the view layer.

If you want to create a new section in the blog showing specific blog posts and their comments, you could easily reuse the comments component.

All in all, this pattern could be considered a specialization of common MVC, and it could come in handy when designing complex systems.

Model–View–ViewModel

The Model-View-ViewModel pattern[5] was created by Microsoft in 2005 as a way to facilitate UI development using WPF and Silverlight; it allows UI developers to write code using a markup language (called XAML) focusing on the User Experience (UX), and accessing the dynamic functionalities using bindings to the code. This approach allows developers and UX developers to work independently without affecting each other's work.

Just like with MVC, the Model in this architecture concentrates the business logic, while the ViewModel acts as a mediator between the Model and the View, exposing the data from the first one. It also contains most of the view logic, allowing the ViewLayer to only focus on displaying information, leaving all dynamic behavior to the ViewModel.

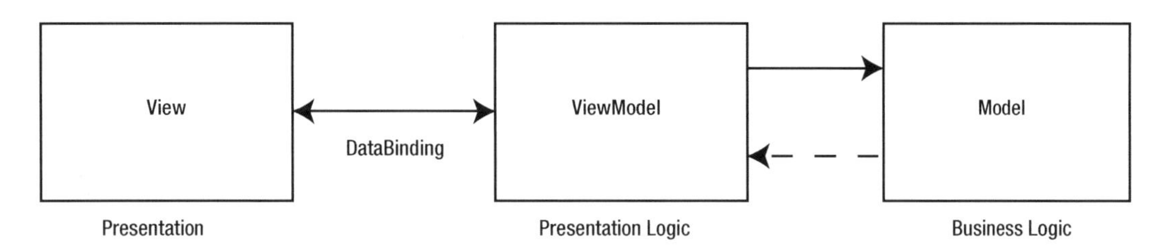

Figure 4-10. *An MVVC architecture*

These days, the pattern has been adopted by others outside Microsoft, like the ZK framework in Java and KnockoutJS, AngularJS, Vue.js, and other frameworks in JavaScript (since MVVM is a pattern specializing in UI development, it makes sense that UI frameworks written in JavaScript are big adopters of this pattern).

Model–View–Adapter

The model-view-adapter[6] (MVA) pattern is very similar to MVC, but with a couple of differences. Mainly, in MVC the main business logic is concentrated inside each model, which also contains the main data structure, with the controller in charge of orchestrating the model and the view.

In MVA, the model is just the data that you're working with, and the business logic is concentrated in the adapter, which is in charge of interacting both with the view and the model. So basically, slimmer models and fatter controllers. But joking aside, this allows for a total decoupling of the view and the model, giving all responsibilities to the adapter.

This approach works great when switching adapters to achieve different behaviors on the same view and model.

The architecture for this pattern is shown in Figure 4-11.

[5]See `http://en.wikipedia.org/wiki/Model_View_ViewModel`.
[6]See `http://en.wikipedia.org/wiki/Model%E2%80%93view%E2%80%93adapter`.

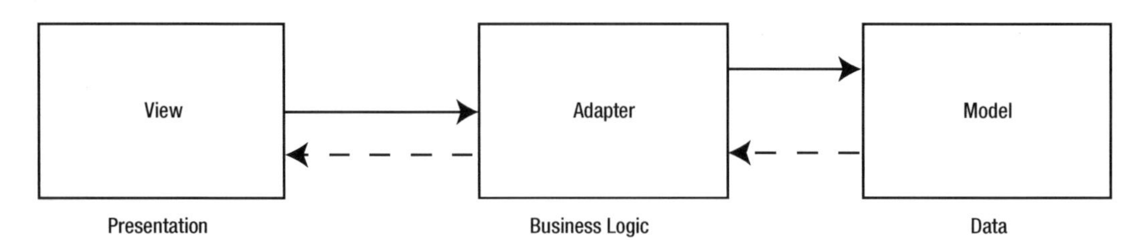

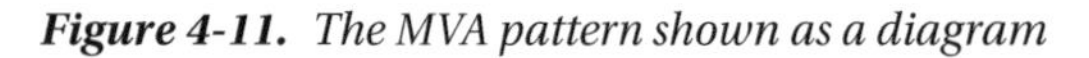

Figure 4-11. *The MVA pattern shown as a diagram*

Response Handler

The final component to our API architecture is the *response handler*; it is in charge of grabbing the resource representation from the view layer and sending it back to the client. The response format (which is not the same as the representation's format) must be the same as the request's format; in this case, it'll be an HTTP 1.1 message.

The HTTP response has two parts: the header, which contains several fields specifying properties about the message, and the body. The content of the message's body is the actual representation of the resource. The header is the section that interests us the most right now; it contains fields like content-type, content-length, and so on. Some of those fields are mandatory and some of them are required if you intend to follow the REST style fully (which you do).

- *Cacheable*: From the constraints imposed by REST defined in Chapter 1. Every request must be explicitly or implicitly set as cacheable when applicable. This translates into the use of the HTTP header `cache-control`.
- *Content-type*: The content type of the response's body is important for the client application to understand how to parse the data. If your resources only have one possible representation, the content type might be an optional header since you could notify the client app developer about the format through your documentation. But if you were to change it in the future, or add a new one, then it might cause some serious damage to your clients. So consider this header mandatory.
- *Status*: The status code is not mandatory but extremely important, as I've mentioned in previous chapters. It provides the client application a quick indicator of the result of the request.
- *Date*: This field should contain the date and time when the message was sent. It should be in HTTP-date format[7] (e.g., Fri, 24 Dec 2014 23:34:45 GMT).
- *Content-length*: This field should contain the number of bytes (length) of the body of the message transferred.

[7]See `http://tools.ietf.org/html/rfc7231#section-7.1.1.1`.

Let's look at an example of an HTTP response with the JSON representation of a resource:

```
HTTP/1.0 200 OK
Date: Fri, 31 Dec 1999 23:59:59 GMT
Content-Type: application/json
Cache-control: private, max-age=0, no-cache
Content-Length: 1354

{
  "name": "J.K.Rolling",
  "id": "ab12351bac",
  "books": [
     {
     "title": "Harry Potter and the Philosopher's Stone",
     "isbn": "9788478888566"
     },
     {
     "title": "Harry Potter and the Prisoner of Azkaban",
     "isbn": "9788422685227"
   }
 ]
}
```

There is one more improvement that could be made on the response handler if you want to get some extra juice. This is entirely extra, and most of the Node.js frameworks out there don't have it (with the exception of Vatican.js).

The idea is to have a post-processing chain of functions that receives the response content returned by the view layer, and transforms it, or enriches it if you will, with further data. It would act as the first version of the pre-processing chain: one common chain for the entire process.

With this idea, you can abstract further code from the controllers just by moving it into the post-processing stage. Code like schema validation (which I'll discuss later in the book) or response header setup can be centralized here, and with the added extra of a simple mechanism for switching it around or disabling steps in the chain.

Let's take a look at the final architecture of our API (see Figure 4-12).

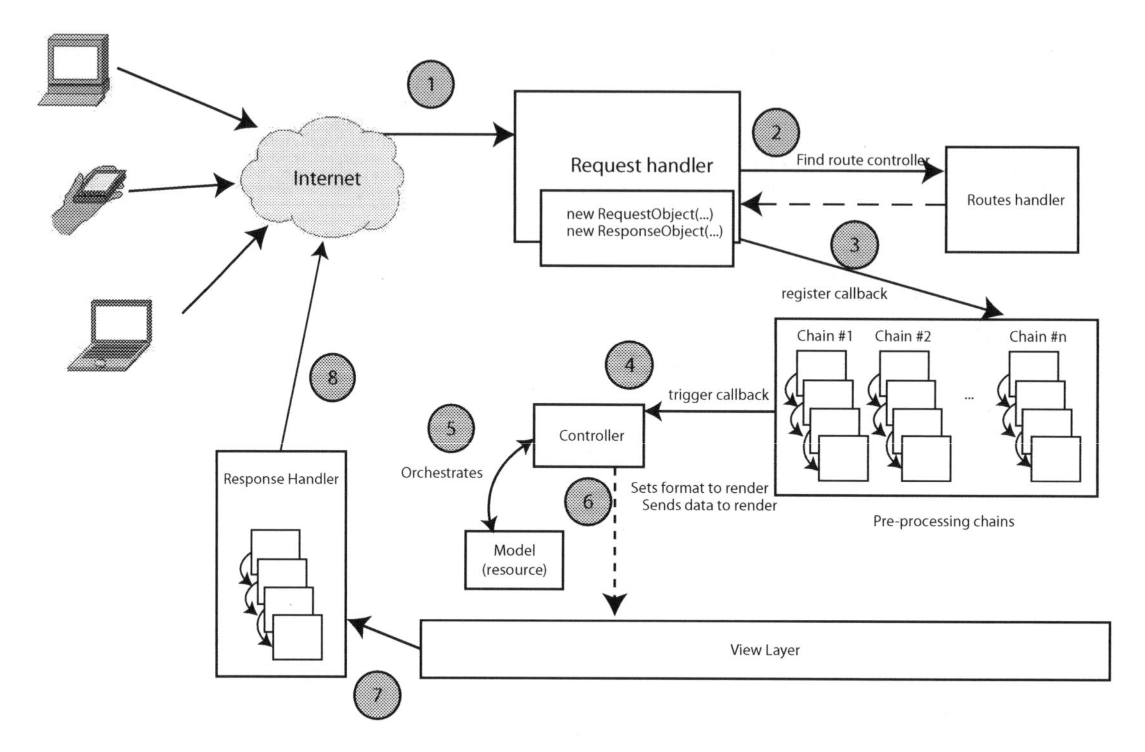

Figure 4-12. *The final architecture with the response handler and the added post-processing chain*

Summary

This chapter covered the basics for a complete and functional RESTful API architecture. It even covered some extras that aren't required but are certainly nice to have, such as pre- and post-processing. You also looked at the main architecture behind our design (MVC) and some alternatives to it, in case your requirements aren't a perfect match for the MVC model.

In the next chapter, I'll start talking about the modules you'll use to write the implementation of this architecture.

CHAPTER 5

Working with Modules

As I discussed in Chapter 3, Node.js has a huge community of developers behind it; they are willing to put hours and effort into providing the rest of the people in that community with high-quality modules. In this chapter, I'll talk about some of those modules; you'll see how to use them to get the architecture described in the Chapter 4.

More specifically, you'll need modules for the following parts:

- *HTTP request and response handling*: This is the most basic feature. As you're about to see, there are plenty of options out there to pick from.
- *Routes handling*: Aside from the preceding, request handling is one of the most important and crucial parts of our system.
- *Pre-processing chain (middleware)*: You can leave out post-processing because it's a less common feature, but pre-processing (or middleware) is common and very useful.
- *Up-to-date documentation*: This wasn't part of our architecture, but I did mention it in Chapter 2, when I talked about good practices. And it so happens that there is a module that will help here, so you might as well add it.
- *Hypermedia on the response*: Again, not part of the architecture, but part of a REST, so you'll add it using the HAL standard.
- *Response and request format validation*: Finally, this will be an added bonus; as a good practice, always validate the format of the requests and responses.

Our Alternatives

Instead of looking at each point individually, you'll take a look at each of the modules, and I'll evaluate them accordingly. Some of them, as you'll see, handle more than just one thing, which sometimes comes in handy because getting unrelated modules to work together is not always an easy task.

Request/Response Handling

Regarding request and response handling, they usually both come in the same module. They are the basics of every HTTP application you intend to make. If you don't know how to handle the HTTP protocol, you can't move forward.

F. Doglio, *Pro REST API Development with Node.js*, DOI 10.1007/978-1-4842-0917-2_5

And because Node.js is such a good fit for HTTP applications, there are quite a few modules that will help you in this task. You need something that can do the following:

- Listen on a specific port for HTTP traffic.
- Translate the HTTP message into a JavaScript object so that you can read it and use it without having to worry about parsing it or about any of the details of the HTTP protocol.
- Write an HTTP response without having to worry about the HTTP message format.

Writing code that listens in a specific port for HTTP traffic is simple; actually, Node.js provides all the tools you need, out of the box, to achieve the three preceding points. Then why do we need extra modules if we can easily do it ourselves? That's a very valid question, and to be honest, it all depends on your needs. If the system you're building is small enough, then it might be a good idea to build the HTTP server yourself; otherwise, it's always good to use a well-tested and tried module. They also solve other related issues for you, such as routes handling, so going with a third-party module might be a good choice.

Routes Handling

Routes handling is tightly coupled with request and response handling; it's the next step in the processing of the request. Once you translate the HTTP message into an actual JavaScript object that you can work with, you need to know which piece of code needs to handle it. This is where routes handling comes in.

There are two sides to this part. First, you need to be able to set up the routes in your code, and associate the handler's code with one or more specific routes. And then the system needs to grab the route of the requested resource and match it to one of yours. That might not be such an easy task. Remember that most routes in any complex system have parameterized parts for things like unique IDs and other parameters. For example, take a look at Table 5-1.

Table 5-1. *Routing Example*

This...	.... needs to match this
`/v1/books/1234412`	`/v1/books/:id`
`/v1/authors/jkrowling/books`	`/v1/:author_name/books`

Usually, routing frameworks provide some sort of templating language that allows developers to set up named parameters in the route template. Later the framework will match the requested URLs to the templates, taking into consideration those variable parts added. Different frameworks add different variations of this; you'll see some of them in a bit.

Middleware

This is the name that the pre-processing chain normally gets in the Node.js world, and that is because the Connect[1] framework (which is the framework most other web frameworks are based on) has this functionality. I already talked about this topic in the previous chapter, so let's look at some examples of middleware functions that are compatible with Connect-based frameworks:

[1]See `https://www.npmjs.com/package/connect`.

```
//Logs every request into the standard output
function logRequests(req, res, next) {
   console.log("[", req.method, "]", req.url)
   next()
}

/**
Makes sure that the body of the request is a valid json object, otherwise, it throws an
error
*/
function formatRequestBody(req, res, next)  {
    if(typeof req.body == 'string') {
      try {
        req.body = JSON.parse(req.body)
     } catch (ex) {
       next("invalid data format")
     }
   }
   next()
}
```

Both examples are different, but at the same time they share a common function signature. Every middleware function receives three parameters: the request object, the response object, and the next function. The most interesting bit here is the last parameter, the next function, calling it is mandatory unless you want to end the processing chain right there. It calls the next middleware in the chain, unless you pass in a value, in which case it'll call the first error handler it finds and it'll pass it the parameter (normally an error message or object).

The use of middleware is very common for things like authentication, logging, session handling, and so forth.

Up-to-Date Documentation

As I've already discussed, keeping up-to-date documentation of the API's interface is crucial if you want developers to use your system. I'll go over some modules that will help in that area. There is no silver bullet, of course; some of modules add more overhead than others, but the main goal is to have some sort of system that updates its documentation as automatically as possible.

Hypermedia on the Response

If you want to follow the REST style to the letter, you need to work this into your system. It is one of the most forgotten features of REST—and a great one, since it allows for self-discovery, another characteristic of a RESTful system.

For this particular case, you'll go with a pre-defined standard called HAL (covered in Chapter 1), so you'll be checking out some modules that allow you to work with this particular format.

Response and Request validation

I'll also go over some modules that will let you validate both the response and the request format. Our API will work with JSON alone, but it's always useful to validate the structure of that JSON in the request due to errors in the client application, and in the response to ensure that there are no errors in the server side after code changes.

Adding a validation on every request might be too big of an overhead, so an alternative might be a test suite that takes care of doing the validation when executed. But the request format validation will have to be done on every request to ensure that the execution of your system is not tainted by an invalid request.

The List of Modules

Now let's go over some modules that take care of one or several of the categories mentioned; for each one, you'll list the following attributes:

- The name of the module
- The category it fits into
- The currently released version
- A small description
- The home page URL
- The installation instructions
- Code examples

We won't compare them because it's not an easy thing to do considering that some modules only handle one thing, whereas others take care of several things. So after going over then, I'll propose a combination of these modules, but you will have enough information to pick a different combo if it fits your problem better.

HAPI

Table 5-2. *HAPI Module Information*

Category	Request/Response handler, Routes handler
Current version	8.1
Description	HAPI is a configuration-centric web framework designed to create any kind of web application, including APIs. The main goal of HAPI is to allow developers to focus on coding the logic of an application, leaving infrastructure code to the framework.
Home page URL	`http://hapijs.com/`

Installation	Installing the framework is simple using npm:
	`$ npm install hapi`
	That's it. HAPI is installed in your application. You can also run the following command to get the dependency added automatically to your `package.json` file:
	`$ npm install --save hapi`

Code Examples

After installation, the most basic thing you can do to initialize the system and get your server up and running is the following:

```
var hapi = require("hapi")

var server = new hapi.Server()
server.connection({ port: 3000 })
server.start(function() {
  console.log("Server running at: ", server.info.url)
})
```

As you can see, this example is quite basic, but the steps required to initialize the application are there. The `server.connection` line returns a server object with the new connection selected. That means you could maintain several open connections at the same time, like this:

```
var Hapi = require('hapi');

var server = new Hapi.Server()
// Create the API server with a host and port
var apiServer = server.connection({
    host: 'localhost',
    port: 8000
});
 //Get list of books for normal client app
apiServer.route({
    method: 'GET',
    path: '/books',
    handler: function(req, reply) {
        //... code to handle this route
    }
})
// Create the Admin  server with a port
var adminServer = server.connection({
    port: 3000
})

//Setup route to get full list of users for admin (with with credential information)
adminSever.route({
    method: 'GET',
    path: '/users',
    handler: function(req, reply) {
        //check credentials...
        //get full list of users...
        //reply(list)
    }
})

server.start(function() {
 console.log("Server started!")
})
```

This code initializes the application, which in turn sets up two different servers: one for the API itself and another one for an admin system. In this code you can also see how easy it is to set up routes with HAPI. Although the code can clearly be cleaned up and the routes definitions can be taken out to a separate file, this is a great example of how two (or more!) servers with their respective routes can be configured using this framework.

Another interesting bit that HAPI provides is the route templates you can use by setting up your own. With it, you can use named parameters, in the following way:

```
var Hapi = require('hapi');
var server = new Hapi.Server();
server.connection({ port: 3000 });

var getAuthor = function (request, reply) {
        // here the author and book parameters are inside
        // request.params
};

server.route({
    path: '/{author}/{book?}',
    method: 'GET',
    handler: getAuthor
});
```

In the preceding code, when setting up the route, anything that's inside curly brackets is considered a named parameter. The last one, has an ? added to it, which means it's optional.

▒ **Note** Only the last named parameter can be set as optional; otherwise, it makes no sense.

In addition to the ?, you can use another special character to tell HAPI the number of segments a named parameter should match; that character is the * and it should be followed by a number greater than 1, or nothing, if you want it to match any number of segments.

▒ **Note** Just like the ? character, only the last parameter can be configured to match any number of segments.

Let's look at some examples:

```
server.route({
    path: '/person/{name*2}',    // Matches '/person/john/doe'
    method: 'GET',
    handler: getPerson
});

server.route({
    path: '/author/{name*}',    // Matches '/author/j/k/rowling' or '/author/frank/herbert'
or /author/
    method: 'GET',
    handler: getAuthor
});
```

```
function getAuthor(req, reply) {
   // The different segments can be obtained like this:
  var segments = req.params.name.split('/')
}
```

Express.js

Table 5-3. *Express.js Module Information*

Category	Request/Response handler, Routes handler, Middleware
Current version	4.11.2
Description	Express is a full-fledged web framework providing small and robust tools for HTTP servers, making it a great candidate for all kinds of web applications, including RESTful APIs.
Home page URL	`http://expressjs.com`
Installation	`$ npm install -g express-generator`

Code Examples

Express.js is sometimes considered the de facto solution when it comes to building a web application in Node.js, much like Ruby on Rails was for Ruby for a long time. That being said, it doesn't mean Express.js should be the only choice or that it is right choice for every project; so make sure that you are well informed before choosing a web framework for your project.

This particular framework has evolved over the years, and now in version 4 it provides a generator. To initialize the entire project, you have to use the following line of code (after installing it as described in Table 5-3):

```
$express ./express-test
```

This line will generate an output like the one shown in Figure 5-1.

```
create : ./express-test
create : ./express-test/package.json
create : ./express-test/app.js
create : ./express-test/public
create : ./express-test/public/javascripts
create : ./express-test/public/images
create : ./express-test/routes
create : ./express-test/routes/index.js
create : ./express-test/routes/users.js
create : ./express-test/public/stylesheets
create : ./express-test/public/stylesheets/style.css
create : ./express-test/views
create : ./express-test/views/index.jade
create : ./express-test/views/layout.jade
create : ./express-test/views/error.jade
create : ./express-test/bin
create : ./express-test/bin/www

install dependencies:
  $ cd ./express-test && npm install

run the app:
  $ DEBUG=express-test:* ./bin/www
```

Figure 5-1. *Output of the express generator command*

The framework generates a lot of folders and files, but in general, it's the structure for a generic web application, one that has views, styles, JavaScript files, and other web app–related resources. This is not for us since we're building a RESTful API. You'll want to remove those folders (views and public, more specifically).

To finalize the process, just enter the folder and install the dependencies; this will leave you with a working web application. Check the `app.js` file if you're curious about what it takes to initialize the framework.

Let's now take a look at what it takes to set up a route in Express.js:

```
//...
var app = express()
//...
app.get('/', function(req, res) {
  console.log("Hello world!")
})
```

That's it. All that you need to remember when setting up a route is the following: app.VERB(URL-TEMPLATE, HANDLER-FUNCTION). The handler function will receive three parameters: the request object, the response object, and the next function. The last parameter is only useful when you set up more than one handler for the same route and method combination; that way you can chain the methods like they are middleware.

Take a look at the following example:

```
app.route('/users/:id')
   .all(checkAuthentication)
   .all(loadUSerData)
   .get(returnDataHandler)
   .put(updateUserHandler)
```

In the preceding code, there are several interesting things happening:

- A named parameter is used for the ID of the user.
- Two middleware functions are set up for every verb hitting the '/users/:id' route.
- It's setting up a handler for the GET method hitting the URL, and at the same time, it's setting up a handler for when the verb is PUT—all in the same line of code.

Express provides its own flavor of named parameters (you saw an example of that in the preceding code), but there are other things you can do. For instance, you can use regular expressions:

```
router.get(/^\/commit\/(\w+)(?:\.\.(\w+))?$/, function(req, res){
  var from = req.params[0];
  var to = req.params[1] || 'HEAD';
  res.send('commit range ' + from + '..' + to);
});
```

The preceding code matches both '/commit/5bc2ab' and '/commit/5bc2ab..57ba31', and you can see that getting the parameter inside the handler's code is simple too.

You can also set a callback function to do some processing when a specific named parameter is received; for instance:

```
var router = express.Router()

router.param('user_id', function(req, res, next, id) {
   loadUser(id, function(err, usr) {
      if(err) {
         next(new Error("There was an error loading the user's information")) //this will
call erorr handler
      } else {
         req.user = usr
         next()
      }
   })

})
//then on the route definition

app.get('/users/:user_id', function(req, res) {
    //req.user is already defined and can be used
})
```

If there is an error on the user_id callback function, then the route's handler will never be called, because the first error handler will be called instead.

Finally, let's look at some examples of middleware usage inside Express.js. I already covered the basics for this type of function earlier, but you never saw how to use it with Express.js. You can do it in two ways: set up a global middleware or a route-specific one.

For a global middleware, you just do this:

```
app.use(function(req, res, next) {
   //your code here will be executed on every request
   next() //remember to call next unless you want the chain to end here.
})
```

For a route-specific middleware, you do this:

```
app.use('/books', function(req, res, next){
        //this function will only be called on this path
        next() //always important to call next unless you don't want the process' flow to
continue.
})
```

You can even set up a route-specific stack of middleware, just by doing this:

```
app.use('/books', function(req, res, next){
    //this function will only be called on this path
    next() //always important to call next unless you don't want the process' flow to continue.
}, function(req, res, next) {
    //as long as you keep calling next, the framework will keep advancing in the chain until
reaching the actual handler
     next()
})
```

Restify

Table 5-4. Restify Module's Information

Category	Request/Response handler, Routes handler, Middleware
Current version	2.8.5
Description	Restify is a framework specifically design for building REST APIs. It borrows heavily from Express.js (specifically, versions prior to 4.0) because Express is considered the standard when it comes to building web apps.
Home page URL	`http://mcavage.me/node-restify/`
Installation	`$ npm install restify`

Code Examples

Restify borrows a lot of its features from Express, so I'll focus on the things that it adds; for other examples, please refer to the previous module or visit the Restify home page.

Initialization is simpler than with Express, although there are no code generators. The following code is all you need to start up a server:

```
var restify = require('restify');

var server = restify.createServer({
   name: 'MyApp',
});

server.listen(8080);
```

The createServer method provides some helpful options that will simplify your job in the future. Table 5-5 lists some of Restify's options.

Table 5-5. *List of Restify Options*

Option	Description
certificate	For building HTTPS servers, pass in the path to the certificate here.
key	For building HTTPS servers, pass in the path to the key file here.
log	Optionally, you can pass in an instance of a logger. It needs to be an instance of node-bunyan.[2]
name	The name of the API. Used to set the server response header; by default it is "restify".
version	A default version for all routes.
formatters	A group of content formatters used for content-negotiation.

In the most basic ways, routes are handled just like Express: you can either pass in the path template and the route handler, or you can pass in a regular expression and the handler.

In a more advanced way, Restify provides some goodies that Express doesn't. The following subsections provide some examples.

Naming Routes

You can set up names for specific routes, which will in turn, allow you to jump from one handler to others using that attribute. Let's look at how to set up the names first:

```
server.get('/foo/:id', function (req, res, next) {
   next('foo2');
});

server.get({
    name: 'foo2',
    path: '/foo/:id'
}, function (req, res, next) {
   res.send(200);
   next();
});
```

[2]See https://github.com/trentm/node-bunyan.

This code is setting up two different handlers for the same path, but Restify will only execute the first handler it finds, so the second one will never get executed unless the `next` statement is called with the name of the second route.

Naming is also used to reference routes when rendering the response, which allows for an interesting feature: hypermedia on the response. To be honest, the solution proposed by Restify is a bit basic and it doesn't really provide a good mechanism for automatically adding hypermedia for self-discovery, but it is more than most other frameworks do. Here is how it works:

```
var restify = require("restify")

var server = restify.createServer()

server.get({
    name: 'country-cities',
    path: '/country/:id/cities'
}, function(req, res, next) {
      res.send('cities')
})

server.get('/country/:id', function(req, res, next) {
  res.send({
    name: "Uruguay",
    cities: server.router.render('country-cities', {id: "uruguay"})
    })
})

server.listen(3000)
```

Versioning Routes

Restify provides support for a global version number, as you saw earlier, but it also provides the ability to have different versions on a per-route basis. And, it also provides support for the *Accept-version* header to pick the right route.

▒ **Note** If the header is missing, and more than one version for the same route is available, Restify will pick the first one defined in the code.

Here is how to do it:

```
function respV1(req, res, next) {
  res.send("This is version 1.0.2")
}
function respV2(req, res, next) {
  res.send("This is version 2.1.3")
}
var myPath = "/my/route"
server.get({path: myPath, version: "1.0.2"},  respV1)
server.get({path: myPath, version: "2.1.3"},  respV2)
```

Now, when hitting the path with different values for Accept-version, the information in Table 5-6 is what you get.

Table 5-6. *Examples of Content Negotiation*

Version Used	Response	Description
	This is version 1.0.2	No version was used, so by default, the server is picking the first one defined.
~1	This is version 1.0.2	Version 1.x.x was selected, so that is what the server responds with.
~3	{ "code": "InvalidVersion", "message": "GET /my/route supports versions: 1.0.2, 2.1.3" }	An error message is returned when an unsupported version is requested.

Content Negotiation

Another interesting feature that Restify provides is support for content negotiation. All you need to do to implement this feature is provide the right content formatters during initialization, like this:

```
restify.createServer({
  formatters: {
    'application/foo; q=0.9': function formatFoo(req, res, body) {
      if (body instanceof Error)
        return body.stack;

      if (Buffer.isBuffer(body))
        return body.toString('base64');

      return util.inspect(body);
    }
  }
})
```

▒ **Note** By default, Restify comes bundled with formatters for application/json, text/plain, and application/octect-stream.

There are other minor features provided by Restify that I'm not covering, so please refer to the official web site for information.

Vatican.js

Table 5-7. Vatican.js Module Information

Category	Request/Response handler, Middleware, Routes handling
Current version	1.3.2
Description	Vatican.js is another attempt of a framework designed to create RESTful APIs. It doesn't follow the Express/Restify path. Its focus is more on the MVP stage of the API, but it provides an interesting alternative.
Home page URL	`http://www.vaticanjs.info`
Installation	`$ npm install -g vatican`

Code Examples

After installation, Vatican.js provides a command-line script to create the project and add resources and resource handlers to it. So to get the project started, you'll need to use the following command:

```
$ vatican new test_project
```

The preceding code generates the output shown in Figure 5-2.

```
New project started:
Creating /home/fernando/workspace/writing/node/test_project ...
Creating /home/fernando/workspace/writing/node/test_project/./handlers ...
Creating /home/fernando/workspace/writing/node/test_project/vatican-conf.json ...
Creating /home/fernando/workspace/writing/node/test_project/index.js ...
Creating /home/fernando/workspace/writing/node/test_project/package.json ...

 Project files created, now just follow these steps:
1- cd into your new project folder
2- npm install
3- node index.js
```

Figure 5-2. Output of the Vatican.js generate action

The main file (index.js) has the following content:

```
var Vatican = require("vatican")

//Use all default settings
var app = new Vatican()

app.dbStart(function() {
    console.log("Db connection stablished...")

    //Start the server
    app.start()
} )
```

Vatican comes with MongoDB integration, so the `dbStart` method is actually a reference to the connection to the NoSQL storage. By default, the server is assumed to be in *localhost* and the database name used is `vatican-project`.

The default port for Vatican is 8753, but just like all defaults in Vatican, it can be overwritten during the instantiation stage. These are the options that can be passed in to the constructor, as shown in Table 5-8.

Table 5-8. *List of Options for the Vatican.js Constructor*

Option	Description
port	Port of the HTTP server.
handlers	Path to the folder where all handlers are stored. By default it's `./handlers`.
db	Object with two attributes: host and dbname.
cors	This is either a Boolean indicating whether CORS is supported by the API, or an object indicating each of the supported headers.

Setting up a route in Vatican is also a bit different than the others; the command-line script provides the ability to autogenerate the code for the entity/model file and the controller/handler file, which also includes basic code for the CRUD operations.

To autogenerate the code, use the following command from within the project's folder:

```
$ vatican g Books -a title:string description:string copies:int -m newBook:post
listBooks:get removeBook:delete
```

This line outputs something like what's shown in Figure 5-3.

```
File written in: /home/fernando/workspace/writing/node/test_project/schemas/Books.js
File written in: ./handlers/Books.js
```

Figure 5-3. *Output of the resource generator command*

It basically means that Vatican created both the handler file and the entity (inside the schemas folder). If you check the handler's file, you'll notice how all the actions already have their code in there; that's because Vatican was able to guess the meaning of the actions provided in the command line by using their name:

- `newBook`: Using "new" assumes you're creating a new instance of the resource.
- `listBooks`: Using "list" assumes you want to generate a list of items.
- `removeBook`: Using "remove" assumes you're trying to remove a resource.

Variations of those words are also valid, and Vatican will use them to guess the code. You can now go ahead and start the server; the endpoints will work and save information to the database.

One final comment on resource generation is about routing; you haven't specified any routes yet, but Vatican has created them anyway. Inside the handler file, you'll notice annotations in the form of the following:

```
@endpoint (url: /books method: post)
BooksHdlr.prototype.newBook = function(req, res, next) {
var data = req.params.body
//...maybe do validation here?
this.model.create(data, function(err, obj) {
    if(err) return next(err)
    res.send(obj)
})
}
```

The annotation above the method's definition is not standard JavaScript, but Vatican is able to parse it and turn it into data during boot up. That means that with Vatican there is no routes file; each route is defined above its associated method, and if you want to get a full list of routes for your system, you can use the following command line:

```
$ vatican list
```

And it'll produce the output shown in Figure 5-4, which lists for every handler all the routes with the method, the path, the file, and the associated method name.

```
2014-12-31T05:18:16.468Z - info: Openning file: ./handlers/Books.js
List of routes found:
[POST] /books -> ./handlers/Books.js::newBook
[GET] /books -> ./handlers/Books.js::listBooks
[DELETE] /books -> ./handlers/Books.js::removeBook
```

Figure 5-4. *Output from the list command*

Note The annotations can be commented out with a single line to avoid your editor/linter from complaining about the construct; even then, Vatican.js will be able to parse it.

Finally, Vatican also fits inside the middleware category, and that's because even though it's not based on Connect or Express, it does support Connect-based middleware. The only difference is the method name that uses it.

```
vatican.preprocess(middlewareFunction) //generic middleware for all routes
vatican.preprocess(middelwareFunction, ['login', 'authentication']) //middleware for two
routes: login and authentication.
```

To set the name of a route, you can add that parameter in the annotation, like this:

```
@endpoint(url: /path method: get name: login)
```

There are still some more features that Vatican.js provides. To read about them, please refer to the official web site.

swagger-node-express

Table 5-9. *swagger-node-express Module Information*

Category	Up-to-date documentation
Current version	2.1.3
Description	This is a module for Express. It integrates into an Express app and provides the functionalities that Swagger[3] does for documenting APIs, which is a web interface with documentation of each method and the ability to try these methods.
Home page URL	`https://github.com/swagger-api/swagger-node-express`
Installation	`$ npm install swagger-node-express`

Code Examples

The first thing you need to do after you install the module is integrate Swagger into your Express app. Here is the code to do that:

```
// Load module dependencies.
var express = require("express")
, app = express()
, swagger = require("swagger-node-express").createNew(app);

// Create the application.
app.use(express.json());
app.use(express.urlencoded());
```

After integration is done, the next thing to do is add the models and the handlers. The models are in the form of JSON data (where this is defined is left to the preference of the developer). The handlers contain the actual code of the route handlers, along with other descriptive fields that act as documentation.

Let's look at an example of a model definition:

```
exports.models = {
        "Book": {
                "id": "Book",
                "required": ["title", "isbn"],
                "properties": {
                                "title": {
                                        "type": "string",
                                        "description": "The title of the book"
                                },
                                "isbn": {
                                        "type": "string",
                                        "description": "International Standard Book Number"
                                },
```

[3]See `http://swagger.io/`.

```
                                    "copies": {
                                            "type": "integer",
                                            "format": "int64",
                                            "description": "Number of copies of the book owned
by the bookstore"
                                    }
                            }
                    }
}
```

As you can see, the format used is JSON Schema[4] and it might be tedious to maintain, but it provides a standard way for Swagger to understand how our models are created.

▒ **Tip** Manually maintaining a lot of model descriptions might be too much work, and it's prone to generate errors in the documentation, so it might be a good idea to either use the description to autogenerate the code of the model, or autogenerate the description from the model's code.

Once the model description is done, you add it to Swagger like this:

```
// Load module dependencies.
var express = require("express")
, swagger = require("swagger-node-express")
, models = require('./models-definitions').models
//....
swagger.addModels(models)
```

Now you move on to the handler's description, which contains fields describing each method, and the actual code to execute.

```
//Book handler's file
exports.listBooks = {
              "spec": {
                            "description": "Returns the list of books",
                            "path": "/books.{format}",
                            "method": "GET",
                            "type": "Book",
                            "nickname": "listBooks",
                            "produces": ["application/json"],
                            "parameters": [swagger.paramTypes.query("sortBy","Sort books
by title or isbn", "string")]
              },
              "action": function(req, res) {
                            //...
              }
}
//main file's code
var bookHandler = require("./bookHandler")
//...
```

[4]See http://json-schema.org/.

```
swagger.addGet(bookHandler.listBooks) // adds the handler for the list action and the actual
action itself
```

This code shows how to describe a specific service (a list of books). Again, some of these parameters (inside the spec object) can be autogenerated; otherwise, manually maintaining a lot of specs can lead to outdated documentation.

Finally, set up the URLs for the Swagger UI (which will display the documentation and will also provide the UI to test the API) and the version:

```
swagger.configure("http://myserver.com", "0.1")
```

Let's now look at a complete example of a main file, showing the setup and configuration of Swagger and the Swagger UI.[5]

```
// Load module dependencies.
var express = require("express")
, models = require("./models").models
, app = express()
, booksHandler = require("./booksHandler") //load the handler's definition
, swagger = require("swagger-node-express").createNew(app) //bundle the app to swagger

// Create the application.
app.use(express.json());
app.use(express.urlencoded());

var static_url = express.static(__dirname + '/ui') //the swagger-ui is inside the "ui"
folder

swagger.configureSwaggerPaths("", "api-docs", "") //you remove the {format} part of the
paths, to simplify things
app.get(/^\/docs(\/.*)?$/ , function(req, res, next) {
    if(req.url === '/docs') {
        res.writeHead(302, {location: req.url + "/"})
        res.end()
        return
    }

    req.url = req.url.substr('/docs'.length)
    return static_url(req, res, next)
})

//add the models and the handler
swagger
    .addModels(models)
    .addGet(booksHandler.listBooks)

swagger.configure("http://localhost:3000", "1.0.0")
app.listen("3000")
```

Figure 5-5 is a screenshot of the resulting UI that you get by visiting `http://localhost:3000/docs`.

[5]See `https://github.com/swagger-api/swagger-ui`.

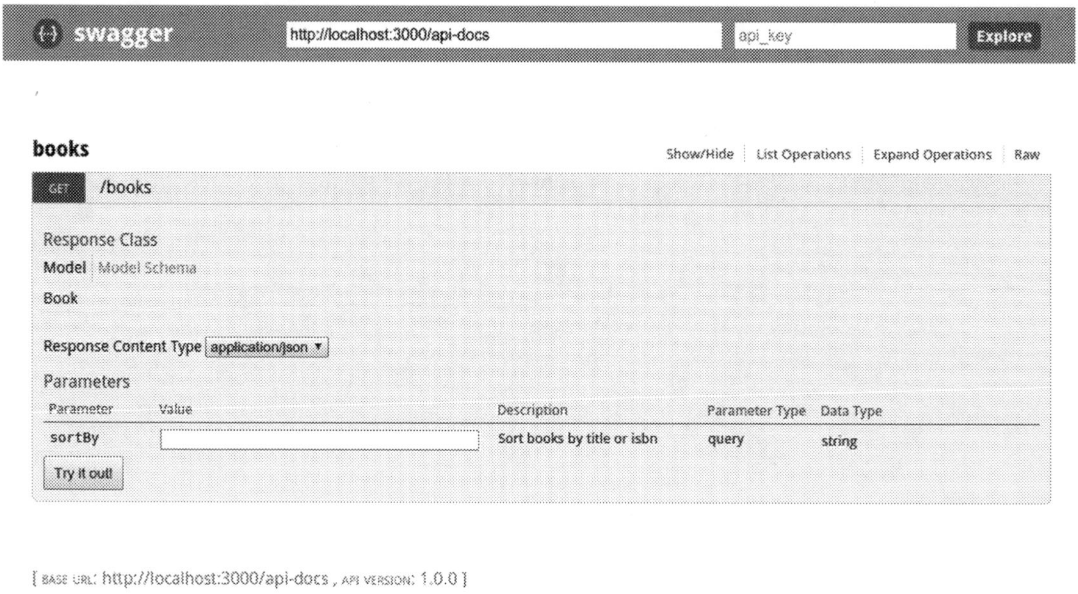

Figure 5-5. *The generated UI*

I/ODocs

Table 5-10. *I/O Docs Module Information*

Category	Up-to-date documentation
Current Version	N/A
Description	I/O Docs is a live documentation system designed for RESTful APIs. By defining the API using the JSON Schema, I/O Docs generates a web interface to try out the API.
Home page URL	`https://github.com/mashery/iodocs`

Installation	`$ git clone http://github.com/mashery/iodocs.git`
	`$ cd iodocs`
	`$ npm install`

Code Examples

After installation is done, the only thing left to do to test the application is create a configuration file; there is a `config.json.sample` file you can use as a starting point.

To start up the documentation server, use one of the following commands:

```
$ npm start       #for *nix and OSX systems
C:\your-project-folder> npm startwin        #for Windows systems
```

After that, use your browser to go to `http://localhost:3000` to start testing the documentation system. Figure 5-6 is a screenshot of one of the sample APIs already configured.

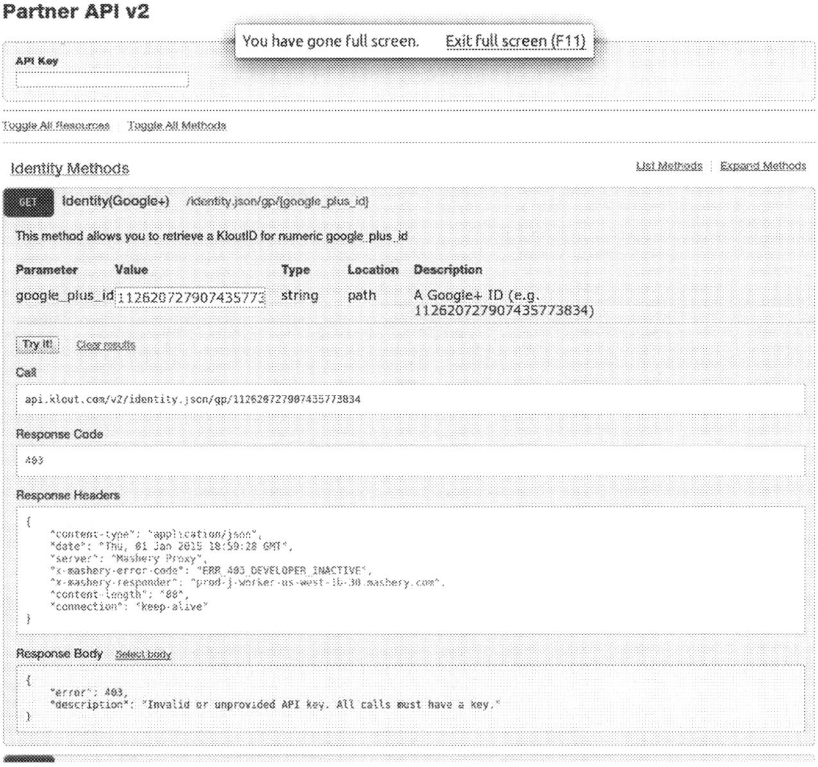

Figure 5-6. *The default UI when trying out methods*

As you can see in Figure 5-6, when the methods are tested, a response is shown underneath. If you want to set up your own API, there are a few things to do:

1. Add your API to the list of documented APIs inside `public/data/apiconfig.json` like this:

```
{
    "klout": {
        "name": "Klout v2 API"
    },
    "egnyte": {
        "name": "Egnyte API"
    },
    "usatoday": {
        "name": "USA TODAY Census API"
    },
    "foursquare": {
        "name": "Foursquare (OAuth 2.0 Auth Code)"
    },
    "rdio": {
        "name": "Rdio Beta (OAuth 2.0 Client Credentials)"
    },
```

```
    "rdio2": {
        "name": "Rdio Beta (OAuth 2.0 Implicit Grant)"
    },
    "requestbin": {
        "name": "Requestb.in"
    },
    "bookstore": {
        "name": "Dummy Bookstore API"
    }
}
```

2. Create a new file called bookstore.json and store it inside the public/data folder. This new JSON file will contain the description of your API and the methods in it; something like this:

```
{
    "name": "Dummy Bookstore API",
    "description": "Simple bookstore API",
    "protocol": "rest",
    "basePath": "http://api.mybookstore.com",
    "publicPath": "/v1",
    "auth": {
        "key": {
                "param": "key"
        }
    },
    "headers": {
        "Accept": "application/json",
        "Foo": "bar"
    },
    "resources": {
        "Books": {
          "methods": {
             "listBooks": {
                "name": "List of books",
                "path": "/books",
                "httpMethod": "GET",
                "description": "Returns the list of books in stock",
                "parameters": {
                   "sortBy": {
                        "type": "string",
                        "required": false,
                        "default": "title",
                        "description": "Sort the results by title or ISBN code"
                   }
                }
             },
                "showBook": {
                   "name": "Show book",
                   "path": "/books/{bookId}",
                   "httpMethod": "GET",
                   "description": "Returns the data of one specific book",
```

```
                    "parameters": {
                       "bookId": {
                           "type": "string",
                           "required": true,
                           "default": "",
                           "description": "The ID of the specific book"
                       }
                    }
              }
            }
          }
       }
    }
```

3. Start up the documentation server and point your web browser to it. You'll see a screen that looks similar to Figure 5-7.

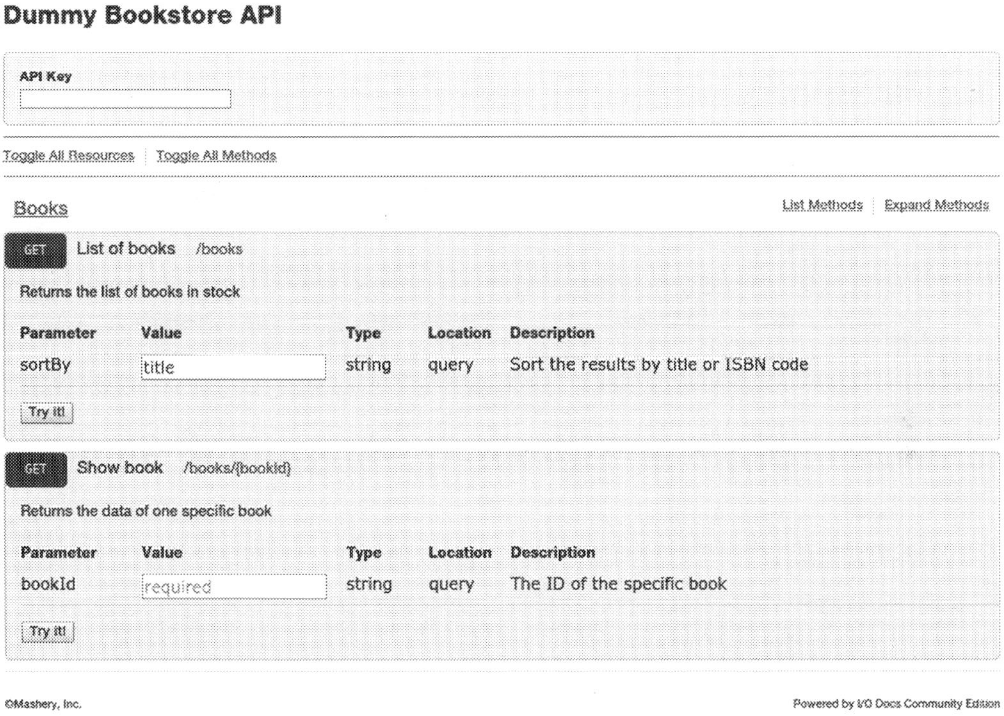

Figure 5-7. *Your custom documentation translated into a web UI*

Unlike with Swagger, this documentation system is not meant to be integrated into your project, so autogenerating the JSON code might be a bit more difficult.

Halson

Table 5-11. Halson Module Information

Category	Hypermedia on the response
Current version	2.3.1
Description	Halson is a module that helps create HAL-compliant JSON objects, which you'll then be able to use as part of the response in your API.
Home page URL	`http://github.com/seznam/halson`
Installation	`$ npm install halson`

Code Examples

The API provided by this module is quite straightforward, and if you've read about the standard,[6] you should have no problem figuring out how to use it.

Here is the example from the readme:

```
var halson = require('halson');

var embed = halson({
        title: "joyent / node",
        description: "evented I/O for v8 javascript"
    })
    .addLink('self', '/joyent/node')
    .addLink('author', {
        href: '/joyent',
        title: 'Joyent'
    });

var resource = halson({
        title: "Juraj Hájovský",
        username: "hajovsky",
        emails: [
             "juraj.hajovsky@example.com",
             "hajovsky@example.com"
        ]
    })
    .addLink('self', '/hajovsky')
    .addEmbed('starred', embed);
console.log(JSON.stringify(resource));
```

The preceding code will output the following:

```
{
  "title": "Juraj Hájovský",
  "username": "hajovsky",
```

[6] See `http://stateless.co/hal_specification.html`.

```
  "emails": [
    "juraj.hajovsky@example.com",
    "hajovsky@example.com"
  ],
  "_links": {
    "self": {
      "href": "/hajovsky"
    }
  },
  "_embedded": {
    "starred": {
      "title": "joyent / node",
      "description": "evented I/O for v8 javascript",
      "_links": {
        "self": {
          "href": "/joyent/node"
        },
        "author": {
          "href": "/joyent",
          "title": "Joyent"
        }
      }
    }
  }
}
```

As you can see, the module successfully abstracted the details about the HAL standard; all you need to know is how to add links and what an embedded object is.

HAL

Table 5-12. *HAL Module Information*

Category	Hypermedia on the response
Current version	0.1.0
Description	HAL is an alternative to HALSON. It provides a simpler interface but the same underlying functionality: abstracting the HAL+JSON format and giving the developer an easy way to use it.
Home page URL	`https://www.npmjs.com/package/hal`
Installation	`$ npm install hal`

Code Examples

The API of this module is simpler than the one provided by HALSON and it also provides XML encoding (remember that even though you're not focusing on XML, it can be a possible second representation for your resources).

Let's look at a simple example following our bookstore theme:

```
var hal = require('hal');

var books = new hal.Resource({name: "Books list"}, "/books")

var listOfBooks = [
  new hal.Resource({id: 1, title: "Harry Potter and the Philosopher's stone", copies: 3}, "/
books/1"),
  new hal.Resource({id: 2, title: "Harry Potter and the Chamber of Secrets", copies: 5}, "/
books/2"),
  new hal.Resource({id: 3, title: "Harry Potter and the Prisoner of Azkaban", copies: 6}, "/
books/3"),
  new hal.Resource({id: 4, title: "Harry Potter and the Goblet of Fire", copies: 1}, "/
books/4"),
  new hal.Resource({id: 5, title: "Harry Potter and the Order of the Phoenix", copies: 8},
"/books/5"),
  new hal.Resource({id: 6, title: "Harry Potter and the Half-blood Prince", copies: 2}, "/
books/6"),
  new hal.Resource({id: 7, title: "Harry Potter and the Deathly Hollows", copies: 7},"/
books/7")
]
books.embed('books', listOfBooks)
console.log(JSON.stringify(books.toJSON()))
```

This code will output the following JSON code:

```
{
  "_links": {
    "self": {
      "href": "/books"
    }
  },
  "_embedded": {
    "books": [
      {
        "_links": {
          "self": {
             "href": "/books/1"
          }
        },
        "id": 1,
        "title": "Harry Potter and the Philosopher's stone",
        "copies": 3
      },
      {
        "_links": {
          "self": {
             "href": "/books/2"
          }
        },
```

```
    "id": 2,
    "title": "Harry Potter and the Chamber of Secrets",
    "copies": 5
  },
  {
    "_links": {
      "self": {
        "href": "/books/3"
      }
    },
    "id": 3,
    "title": "Harry Potter and the Prisoner of Azkaban",
    "copies": 6
  },
  {
    "_links": {
      "self": {
        "href": "/books/4"
      }
    },
    "id": 4,
    "title": "Harry Potter and the Goblet of Fire",
    "copies": 1
  },
  {
    "_links": {
      "self": {
        "href": "/books/5"
      }
    },
    "id": 5,
    "title": "Harry Potter and the Order of the Phoenix",
    "copies": 8
  },
  {
    "_links": {
      "self": {
        "href": "/books/6"
      }
    },
    "id": 6,
    "title": "Harry Potter and the Half-blood Prince",
    "copies": 2
  },
  {
    "_links": {
      "self": {
        "href": "/books/7"
      }
    },
```

```
        "id": 7,
        "title": "Harry Potter and the Deathly Hollows",
        "copies": 7
      }
    ]
  },
  "name": "Books list"
}
```

JSON-Gate

Table 5-13. *JSON-Gate Module Information*

Category	Request/Response validation
Current version	0.8.22
Description	This module validates the structure and content of a JSON object against a predefined schema that follows the JSON Schema format.
Home page URL	`https://www.npmjs.com/package/json-gate`
Installation	`$ npm install json-gate`

Code Examples

The usage of this module is quite simple. First, you need to define the schema against which your objects will be validated. This can be done directly with the `createSchema` method or (recommended) in a separate file, and then passed to the validator. After the schema has been added, you can proceed to validate as many objects as you need.

Here is a simple example:

```
var createSchema = require('json-gate').createSchema;

var schema = createSchema({
    type: 'object',
    properties: {
        title: {
                type: 'string',
                minLength: 1,
                maxLength: 64,
                required: true
        },
        copies: {
                type: 'integer',
                maximum: 20,
                default: 1
        },
        isbn: {
                type: 'integer',
                required: true
        }
```

```
    },
    additionalProperties: false
});

var invalidInput = {
    title: "This is a valid long title for a book, it might not be the best choice!",
    copies: "3"
}

try {
   schema.validate(invalidInput);
} catch(err) {
    return console.log(err)
}
```

The preceding code will output the following error:

```
[Error: JSON object property 'title': length is 71 when it should be at most 64]
```

There are two things to note here:

- On one hand, the error message is very "human friendly." All the error messages reported by JSON-Gate are like this, so it's easy to understand what you did wrong.
- On the other hand, as you probably noticed, the `invalidInput` object has two errors in its format; the validation stops at the first error, so correcting multiple problems might be slow because you'll have to correct them one at a time.

If you're not into catching exceptions (and why should you in Node.js?), there is an alternative to the `validate` method, which is passing in a second argument—a callback function with two arguments: the error object and the original input object.

TV4

Table 5-14. *TV4 Module Information*

Category	Request/Response validation
Current version	1.1.9
Description	This module provides validation against version 4 of the JSON Schema.[7]
Home page url	`https://www.npmjs.com/package/tv4`
Installation	`$ npm install tv4`

Code Examples

The main difference between this validator and JSON-Gate is that this one is specific for version 4 of the JSON Schema draft. It also allows you to collect multiple errors during validation and to reference other schemas, so you can reuse parts of the schema in different sections.

[7]See `http://json-schema.org/latest/json-schema-core.html`.

Let's look at some examples:

```
var validator = require("tv4")

var schema ={
    "title": "Example Schema",
    "type": "object",
    "properties": {
        "firstName": {
            "type": "string"
        },
        "lastName": {
            "type": "string"
        },
        "age": {
            "description": "Age in years",
            "type": "integer",
            "minimum": 0
        }
    },
    "required": ["firstName", "lastName"]
}

var invalidInput = {
    firstName: 42,
    age: "100"

}
var results = validator.validateMultiple(invalidInput, schema)
console.log(results)
```

The preceding example will output the following error object:

```
{ errors:
   [ { message: 'Missing required property: lastName',
       params: [Object],
       code: 302,
       dataPath: '',
       schemaPath: '/required/1',
       subErrors: null,
       stack: '......'},
     { message: 'Invalid type: number (expected string)',
       params: [Object],
       code: 0,
       dataPath: '/firstName',
       schemaPath: '/properties/firstName/type',
       subErrors: null,
       stack: '......'},
     { message: 'Invalid type: string (expected integer)',
       params: [Object],
       code: 0,
```

```
      dataPath: '/age',
      schemaPath: '/properties/age/type',
      subErrors: null,
      stack: '......'}]
  missing: [],
  valid: false }
```

The output is much bigger than the one from JSON-Gate and it needs a bit of parsing before being able to use it, but it also provides quite a lot of information aside from the simple error message.

For a full reference on the API provided by this validator, please visit its home page. To understand the all the possible validations that can be done using JSON Schema, please visit the online draft.

Summary

This chapter covered a lot of modules that will help you create the perfect API architecture. You saw at least two modules for every category on options for picking the tools for the job.

In the next chapter, you'll define the API that you'll be developing in the following chapters, and with that definition, you'll also pick the set of modules (from the list in this chapter) that you'll use to develop it.

CHAPTER 6

Planning Your REST API

You're almost ready to get your hands dirty and start developing the actual API; but before you start, let's apply everything I've talked about until this point:

- REST
- Defining what an ideal RESTful architecture should look like
- Good practices when developing an API
- Modules that would help achieve that ideal goal

In this chapter, I'll set up the ground work for the final development this book will take you through:

- I'll define a specific problem to solve.
- You'll create a written specification for it, writing down the list of resources and endpoints.
- To help understand how all those resources relate to each other, you'll create a UML diagram of our system.
- I'll go over some options for a database engines, choosing the best one for our problem.

The final result of this chapter will be all the information you need to start the development process (covered in the next chapter).

The Problem

In case you haven't noticed yet, throughout this book, every major (and probably minor too) code sample and fake scenario has been done using a bookstore as root of that example. This chapter keeps up that trend, so instead of switching into another area, you'll dig deeper and flesh-out our fake bookstore.

Let's call our fake bookstore Come&Read and assume that we've been asked to create a distributed API that will bring the bookstore into the twenty-first century.

Right now, it's a pretty decent business. The bookstore currently has 10 different points of sale located across the United States; not a lot, but the company leadership is considering expanding into even more states. The current main problem, though, is that all of those stores have barely entered the digital era. The way of working and recordkeeping is very manual and heterogeneous; for instance:

- Some of the smaller stores keep records on paper and send a manually typed weekly report to the head store.
- While the bigger locations tend to use some sort of CRM software, there is no standard as long as numbers are exported into a common format and sent in a weekly report.

F. Doglio, *Pro REST API Development with Node.js*, DOI 10.1007/978-1-4842-0917-2_6

- Based on the weekly reports, the head store handles inventory of the chain-wide matters (store-specific stock, global stock, sales both per-store and global, employee records, etc.).
- Overall, the bookstore lacks web interaction with its customers, which a twenty-first century business must have. Its web site only lists addresses and phone numbers, and nothing more.

An image mapping the current situation of this bookstore chain is shown in Figure 6-1.

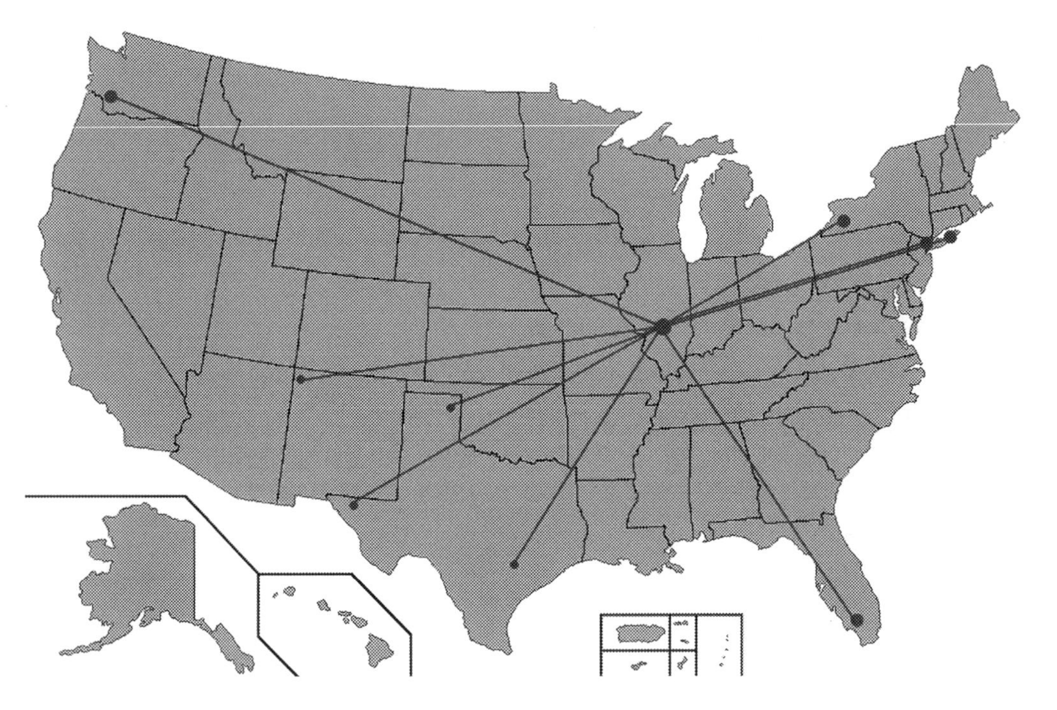

Figure 6-1. *How every store connects to the main store*

As you can see in Figure 6-1, all of the secondary stores are connected by a very thin line to the main store, which is located in Springfield, IL.

The goal is to grow as a business, by not only opening new stores across the country but by also strengthening the bond between all the stores. And to achieve this, the backbone of everything will be our API. Our system will have to be a decentralized one, meaning that you'll treat the main store just like any other store, and provide a common set of tools and data sources for every client application that might come in the future, instantly allowing for such things as the following:

- Cross-store searches
- Automatic control of global stock
- Automatic control over sales on a global level
- Dynamic data sources for things like web sites and mobile apps

A new mental image of this bookstore chain might be like the one shown in Figure 6-2.

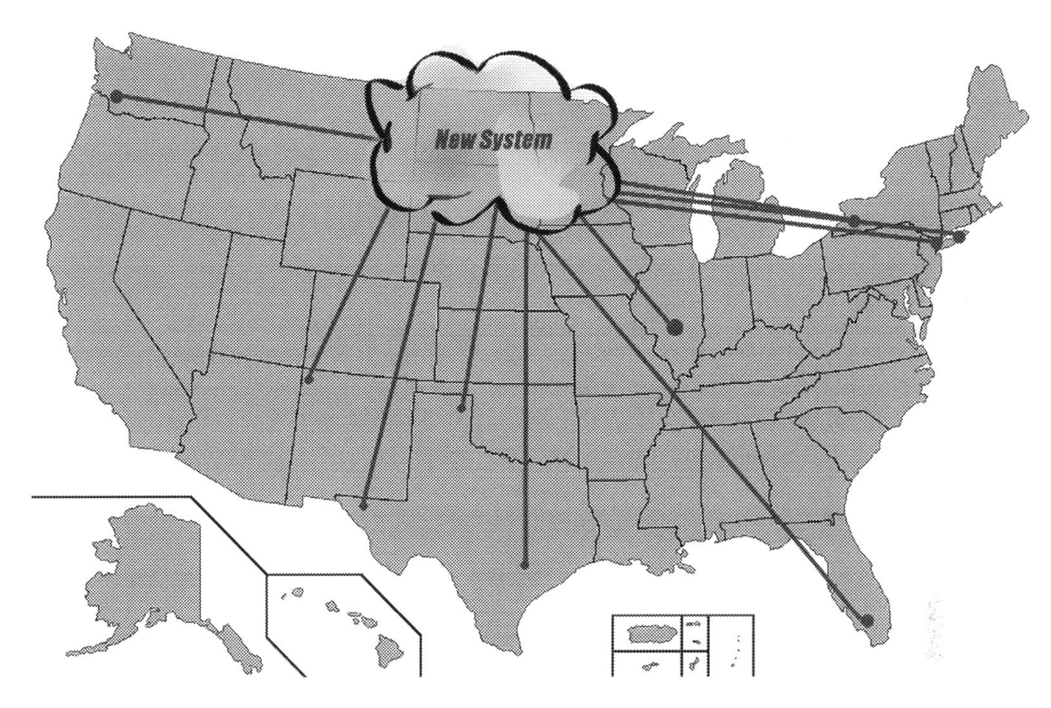

Figure 6-2. *The new status of the bookstore chain*

Figure 6-2 shows the new system living in the cloud, with all stores connected directly to it. The bond is stronger now, since everything is done automatically and every piece of information is available to all stores. Also, this new API-based system allows for the easy development of new ways to interact with potential customers, including mobile apps and dynamic web sites.

The Specifications

Now that we know the current situation of the chain and the goal of our system, we need to start writing some hard specs. These will determine the way the system evolves and help with planning the development by giving us a better idea of the size of the project. Specifications also help us spot any design errors before we start with the implementation.

▒ **Note** We will not spend much time on the process of writing the system's specs, since that subject is beyond the scope of this book. We'll just lay down the specs and note anything that might be extremely relevant; the rest will be left to your understanding of this process.

To provide everything mentioned, the system needs to have the following features:

- *Cross-store book search/listing capabilities.*
- *Storage*: This code is in charge of providing the information to all other entities, as well as talking directly to the data storage system that you choose.

- *Sales*: This feature is dedicated to allow for both in-store and online sales.
- *User reviews of books*: This will provide a much-needed layer of interaction between the stores and the potential clients.
- *Authentication*: For store employees and for customers.

Table 6-1 describes the resources that we'll be dealing with in this implementation.

Table 6-1. *Resources, Properties, and Basic Descriptions*

Resource	Properties	Description
Books	• Title • Authors • ISBN Code • Stores • Genre • Description • Reviews • Price	This is the main entity; it has all the properties required to identify a book and to locate it in a specific store.
Authors	• Name • Description • Books • Website • Image/Avatar	This resource is highly related to a book's resource because it lists the author of every book in a store.
Stores	• Name • Address • State • Phone numbers • Employees	Basic information about each store, including the address, employees, and so forth.
Employees	• First name • Last name • Birthdate • Address • Phone numbers • Email • HireDate • EmployeeNumber • Store	Employee information, contact data, and other internal properties that may come in handy for an admin type of user.
Clients	• Name • Address • Phone number • Email	Basic contact information about a client.
BookSales	• Date • Books • Store • Employee • Client • TotalAmount	The record of a book sale. It can be related to a store sale or an online sale.

(*continued*)

Table 6-1. (*continued*)

Resource	Properties	Description
ClientReviews	• Client • Book • ReviewText • Stars	The resource in which client reviews about a book is saved. The client can enter a short free-text review and a number between 0 and 5 to represent stars.

Note Even though it's not listed in Table 6-1, all resources will have some database-related attributes, such as `id`, `created_at`, and `updated_at`, which you'll use throughout the code.

Based on the resources in Table 6-1, let's create a new table that lists the endpoints needed for each resource. Table 6-2 helps define the functionalities that each resource will have associated to it.

Table 6-2. List of Endpoints, Associated Parameters, and HTTP Methods

Endpoint	Attributes	Method	Description
`/books`	`q`: Optional search term. `genre`: Optional filtering by book genre. Defaults to "all".	GET	Lists and searches all books. If the `q` parameter is present, it's used as a free-text search; otherwise, the endpoint can be used to return lists of books by genre.
`/books`		POST	Creates a new book and saves it in the database.
`/books/:id`		GET	Returns information about a specific book.
`/books/:id`		PUT	Updates the information on a book.
`/books/:id/authors`		GET	Returns the author(s) of a specific book.
`/books/:id/reviews`		GET	Returns user reviews for a specific book.
`/authors`	`genre`: Optional; defaults to "all". `q`: Optional search term.	GET	Returns a list of authors. If `genre` is present, it's used to filter by the type of book published. If `q` is present, it's used to do a free- text search on the author's information.
`/authors`		POST	Adds a new author.
`/authors/:id`		PUT	Updates the data on a specific author.
`/authors/:id`		GET	Returns the data on a specific author.
`/authors/:id/books`		GET	Returns a list of books written by a specific author.
`/stores`	`state`: Optional; filters the list of stores by state name.	GET	Returns the list of stores.

(*continued*)

Table 6-2. *(continued)*

Endpoint	Attributes	Method	Description
/stores		POST	Adds a new store to the system.
/stores/:id		GET	Returns the data on a specific store.
/stores/:id/books	q: Optional; does a full-text search of books within a specific store. genre: Optional; filters the results by genre.	GET	Returns a list of books that are in stock at a specific store. If the attribute q is used, it performs a full-text search on those books.
/stores/:id/employees		GET	Returns a list of the employees working at a specific store.
/stores/:id/booksales		GET	Returns a list of the sales at a specific store.
/stores/:id		PUT	Updates the information about a specific store.
/employees		GET	Returns a full list of the employees working across all stores.
/employees		POST	Adds a new employee to the system.
/employees/:id		GET	Returns the data on a specific employee.
/employees/:id		PUT	Updates the data on a specific employee.
/clients		GET	Lists clients ordered alphabetically by name.
/clients		POST	Adds a new client to the system.
/clients/:id		GET	Returns the data on a specific client.
/clients/:id		PUT	Updates the data on a specific client.
/booksales	start_date: Filters records that were created after this date. end_date: Optional; filters records that were created before this date. store_id: Optional; filters records by store.	GET	Returns a list of sales. The results can be filtered by time range or by store.
/booksales		POST	Records a new book sale.
/clientreviews		POST	Saves a new client review of a book.

▒ **Tip** Even though they're not specified, all endpoints that deal with listing resources will accept the following attributes: `page` (starting at 0, the page number to return); `perpage` (the number of items per page to return); and a special attribute called `sort`, which contains the field name by which to sort the results and the order in the following format: [FIELD_NAME]_[ASC|DESC] (e.g., title_asc).

Table 6-2 gives us a pretty good idea of the size of the project; with it we're able to estimate the amount of work that we have ahead of us.

There is one more aspect to discuss because it isn't covered in the resources in Table 6-1 or with the endpoints/authentication in Table 6-2.

The authentication scheme will be simple. As discussed in Chapter 2, we'll use the *stateless* alternative by signing every request with a MAC (message authentication code). The server will re-create that code to verify that the request is actually valid. This means there will not be a signing process embedded into our system; that can be done by the client. No need to worry about that for now.

▒ **Note** Since it's not part of the scope of this book, the API will not handle charging for the book sales. This means that we'll assume that the book sale was done outside of our system, and that another system will post the results into our API to keep a record of it. In a production system, this is a good way to handle this functionality inside the API itself, thus providing a complete solution.

Keeping Track of Stock per Store

Table 6-1 shows that every book tracks which stores it is being sold at. What is not completely clear, however, is what happens if there is more than one copy of the same book per store.

To keep track of this number, let's enhance the relation between the books and the stores models by assigning another element: the number of copies. You'll see this in a bit in the UML diagram, but this is how the system will keep global stock of every book.

UML Diagram

With the level of specification we have so far, we could very well skip this step and jump right into the next one; but for the sake of completeness and getting a clear idea across, let's create a basic UML diagram to provide another way to show how all of the resources of the API will relate to each other.

As you can see in Figure 6-3, most of the diagram consists of groups of aggregations between different resources. The store has a group for employees, a group for books, a group for the books' authors (usually it's one author per book, but there are books that are co-authored by two or more authors), and a group for client reviews.

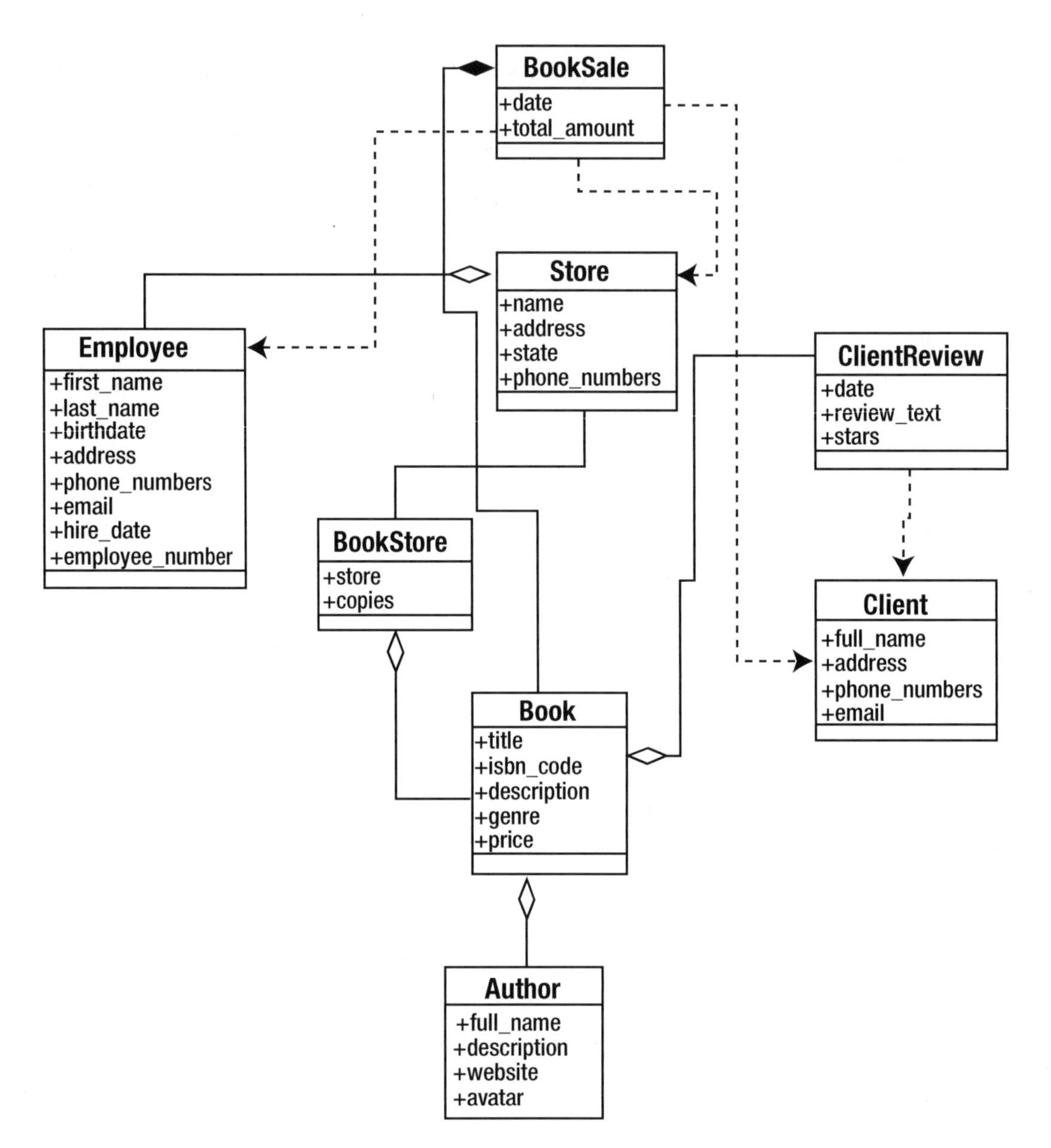

Figure 6-3. *UML diagram showing the relations between all resources*

Choosing a Database Storage System

It's time to stop writing lists of endpoints and creating diagrams; you need to start picking technologies. In this case, I'll go over some of the most common choices for a database storage system. I'll talk a bit about each one and we'll decide on one of them.

The bottom line is that all the solutions are valid—you could very well go with any of them, but we'll need to choose one in the end, so let's define what it is needed in the database system:

- *Speed of development*: Because you want the process to go quickly and not have interaction with the database be a bottleneck, you need something that integrates easily.
- *Easy-to-change schema*: With everything predefined, you have a pretty solid idea of what the schema is going to look like, but you might want to adjust things during development. It's always better if the storage you're using allows for this without a lot of hustle.
- *Ability to handle entity relations*: This means that key/value stores are out of the question.
- *Seamless integration between the entities' code and the database representation of the data.*

That's pretty much about it. In this case, we want something that can be integrated fast, changed easily, and is not key/value.

Therefore, the options are as follows:

- MySQL[1]: A classic choice when it comes to relational databases.
- PostgreSQL[2]: Another great choice when it comes to relational database engines.
- MongoDB[3]: A document-based NoSQL database engine.

So, now that you have our list of options, let's analyze how well each one of them complies with our requirements.

Fast Integration

Integration with the system means how easily the modules interact with the specific database engine. With MySQL and PostgreSQL, there is Sequelize,[4] which provides very complete and powerful object-relational mapping (ORM). It lets you focus more on the data model than on the actual engine particularities. Besides, if you use it right, you can potentially switch between both engines with minimum impact on the code.

On the other hand, with MongoDB you have Mongoose.js,[5] which allows you to abstract your code from the engine, simplifying your task when it comes to defining the schemas, validations, and so forth.

Easy-to-Change Schemas

This time around, the fixed structure provided by both MySQL and PostgreSQL makes it harder to maintain dynamic schemas, so every time you make a change, you'll need to update the schema by running migrations.

The lack of structure provided by the NoSQL engines makes MongoDB the perfect choice for our project, because making a change on the schema is as simple as making the changes on the definition code; no migration or anything else required.

---

[1]See `http://mysql.com/`.
[2]See `http://www.postgresql.org/`.
[3]See `http://www.mongodb.org/`.
[4]See `http://sequelizejs.com/`.
[5]See `http://mongoosejs.com/`.

Ability to Handle Entity Relations

Since we're leaving out key/value stores like Redis,[6] all of our three options are able to handle entity relations. Both MySQL and PostgreSQL are especially good at this, since they're both *relational* database engines. But let's not rule out MongoDB; it is *document*-based NoSQL storage, which in turn allows you to have documents (that translate directly into a MySQL record) and subdocuments, which are a special kind of relation that we don't have with our relational options.

Subdocument relations help to simplify both schemas and queries when working with the data. You saw in Figure 6-3 that most of our relations are based on aggregation, so this might be a good way to solve that.

Seamless Integration Between Our Models and the Database Entities

This is more of a comparison between Sequelize and Mongoose. Since they both abstract the storage layer, you need compare how that abstraction affects this point.

Ideally, we want our entities (our resources' representations in the code) to be passed to our storage layer or to interact with the storage layer. We don't want to require an extra type of object, usually called a DTO (data transfer object), to transfer the state of our entities between layers.

Luckily, the entities provided by Sequelize and by Mongoose fall into this category, so we might as well call it a draw.

And the Winner Is...

We need to pick one, so let's summarize:

- *Fast integration*: Let's give this one to Sequelize, since it comes with the added bonus of being able to switch engines with minimum impact.
- *Easy-to-change schemas*: MongoDB wins this one, hands down.
- *Handling of entity relations*: I'd like to give this one to MongoDB as well, mainly due to the subdocuments feature.
- *Seamless integration with our data models*: This one is a draw, so we're not counting it.

The final result seems to point toward MongoDB, but it's a pretty close win, so in the end, personal experience needs to be taken into account as well. Personally, I find MongoDB to be a very interesting alternative when prototyping and creating something new, something that might change during the development process many times, but this is why we'll go with it for our development. This way there is the extra insurance that if we need to change something, like adapting our data model to a new structure, we can do so easily and with minor impact.

The obvious module choice here is Mongoose, which provides a layer of abstraction over the MongoDB driver.

Choosing the Right Modules for the Job

This is the last step of our preparation process. Now that you know the problem to solve and you have a pretty well-defined specification of how to handle the development, the only thing left to do, aside from actually coding, is to pick the right modules.

---

[6]See `http://redis.io`.

In the previous chapter, I went over a list of modules that would help us achieve a pretty complete RESTful system; so let's quickly pick some of them for this development:

- Restify will be the basis of everything we do. It'll provide the structure needed to handle and process the requests and to provide a response to them.
- Swagger will be used to create the documentation. In the previous chapter, I talked about swagger-node-express, but just like that, there is one that works with Restify called (unsurprisingly enough) swagger-node-restify.[7] This module was chosen because it integrates into our project, allowing us to autogenerate our documentation based on our original code, instead of having to maintain two different repositories.
- Halson will be our module of choice for adding hypermedia to our responses. Mainly chosen because it appears to be more mature than HAL (the other modules examined for this task).
- Finally, the validation of our JSONs will be done using TV4, mainly because it allows us to gather all validation errors at once.

▒ **Note** These are not the only modules that we'll use; there are other minor auxiliary modules that will help us in different situations, but the ones listed are the ones that will help us achieve a RESTful API.

Summary

We now have all we need to start coding. We know the extent of the API for the bookstore chain that we'll develop. We have planned the internal architecture of the system and have chosen the main modules that we'll use.

In the next chapter, we'll start coding our API. By the end of the chapter, we should have a full-fledged working bookstore API.

[7]See `https://www.npmjs.com/package/swagger-node-restify`.

CHAPTER 7

Developing Your REST API

Now that we have finally defined the tools that we'll use and the project that we'll develop with them, we're ready to actually start coding. This chapter will cover that part—from the organization of the files (the directory structure), through the small design decisions made during development, and finally to the code itself.

This chapter will display the entire source code for the project, but we'll only go over the relevant parts. Sadly, some bits and pieces are just plain boring (like the JSON Schema definitions and the simpler models), so I'll skip it. These things should be pretty self-explanatory to developers anyway, no matter the level of expertise.

I'll cover the development stage as follows:

- Minor simplifications/design decisions made during development.
- Folder structure, because it's always important to understand where everything is and why.
- The code itself, file by file, including explanation when needed.

Note The code in this chapter is but one of the infinitely potential ways of solving the problem presented in Chapter 6. It attempts to show the concepts and modules mentioned throughout this book. It's also meant to show you only one potential development process, which tries to be agile and dynamic at the same time. Of course, there are different ways to go about the process, which may be better or worse for every reader.

Minor Changes to the Plan

We spent two whole chapters going over different modules and planning the entire process to develop the API. We made some diagrams, and we even listed every resource and endpoint that we would need.

And yet, during development, the plan changes. Not by a lot, but we still need to fine-tune some aspects of the design.

This isn't necessarily a bad thing, though. If the original plan changes significantly, then yes, that would mean we definitely did something wrong in the planning; but there is no escape from minor changes at this stage, unless you spend a lot more time in your design phase. I'm talking about going the whole nine yards here: writing detailed use cases with their corresponding edge conditions, flow charts—the works. That process—when done right and when followed by the team implementing the solution—most likely results in no changes during development. But for that to happen, we need a lot more time, and let's face it, aside from

F. Doglio, *Pro REST API Development with Node.js*, DOI 10.1007/978-1-4842-0917-2_7

being the boring part of development (disclaimer: if you actually like that part better than developing, there's nothing wrong with you; I just haven't ever met anyone like you), it's not this book's focus either.

So we can play with the design, use the partial analysis and planning that we did in the previous chapter, and live with the consequences, which are very little, as you'll see.

Simplification of the Store: Employee Relationship

When I listed every resource, I said that the store would keep a list of employees and that each employee would keep a direct reference to the store. To maintain those relationships in MongoDB, however, means extra work. And since we don't really need this, we'll just keep the employees' records unaware of their assigned store, and make sure that each store keeps up with the employees working in it.

Adding Swagger UI

I talked about Swagger back in Chapter 5, and I briefly mentioned Swagger UI, but I never really explained a lot. The Swagger UI project is the UI we'll use to test our API. The swagger-node-express and swagger-node-restify modules provide the back-end infrastructure that the UI needs; but without the Swagger UI project, we have nothing.

So, just download it (or clone the repo) from `https://github.com/swagger-api/swagger-ui` and add it into your project. I'll go over how to configure it in a bit.

Simplified Security

To will simplify the security, we'll work under the premise that we're not really making a public API but rather an API for clients that are directly under our control.

That means that we will not require every client to request an access token with a limited life span. Instead, we'll work under the assumption that when we set up a new client in a new branch, we share the secret passphrase; so clients will always send the MAC code encrypted using this passphrase, and the API will rehash each request to make sure both results match. This way we're still validating the requests and we remain true to REST, because this method is stateless; we're just not simplifying the addition of new client applications.

To explain a bit further, each client will send, on every request, two very specific pieces of information:

- A special header called `hmacdata` with the information being encrypted.
- The `api_key` parameter with the value of the encryption result.

Upon receiving the request, the API will grab the data from the header and encrypt it again, using the correct passphrase. If the result is the same as the value of the `api_key` parameter, then it'll dim the request as authentic. Otherwise, it'll reject the request with a 401 error code.

A Small Backdoor for Swagger

The other change that we're making is because the Swagger UI has no de facto support for our authentication scheme. We can send a fixed `api_key` parameter, but we would have to change the code of the client to get it to use the same algorithm we're using. This is why we've added a small backdoor in our code to let the Swagger UI go by without needing to authenticate each request.

The hack is very simple. Since the UI can send a fixed `api_key`, we'll let all requests that have an `api_key` equal to 777 pass, automatically trusting them. This backdoor will need to be removed when going into production to avoid any security issues, of course.

MVC

In Chapter 4, I went over several variations of the MVC pattern, but never actually settled on one to be used on our API. Personally, I really liked the idea behind Hierarchical MVC, since it allows for some really clean code. That said, it also means extra work when developing. And considering that there aren't many cases where in one controller we're dealing with resources from another, we'll try to keep it simple and go with a basic MVC.

This means that we'll have the following key elements in our project:

- *Controllers*: Handles requests and calls upon the models for further action.
- *Models*: Holds the main logic of the API. Since in our simple case that logic is basically querying the database, these will be the models used by Mongoose. This will simplify our architecture. Also, Mongoose provides different mechanisms to add extra behaviors to our models (things like setting instance methods or post-action hooks).
- *View*: The view will be embedded inside the model's code in the form of a method that translates the specifics of one model into a HAL + JSON that can be returned back to the client.

Folder Structure

To completely understand the design behind our API, let's quickly take a look at the folder structure that I've set up (see Figure 7-1).

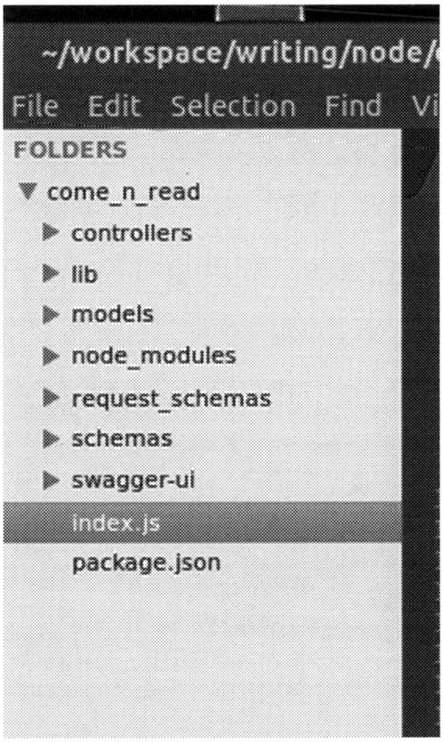

Figure 7-1. *Project folder structure*

Here are the folders we'll be creating and using:

- `controllers`: This folder contains the code for our controllers. It also has an `index.js` file to handle exporting the contents of the rest of them. There is also a base controller here, which contains all the generic methods that all controllers should have; so every new controller can extend this and inherit said methods.
- `lib`: This folder contains the miscellaneous code not big enough to have its own folder, but required across several different places in our project; for instance, database access, helper functions, the config files, and so forth.
- `models`: Inside this folder are the model files. Normally when working with Mongoose, a model's file has the schema definition, and you return the instantiation of that schema as your model. In our case, the actual definition is somewhere else, so this code handles loading that external definition, adding the extra behavior specific to each model, and then returning it.
- `request_schemas`: Inside this folder are the JSON Schemas used to validate the different requests.
- `schemas`: These are the JSON Schemas of the models, used for the Swagger module to define the UI for testing and for the Mongoose model's definition. We will have to add some code to translate from the first one to the latter, since they don't use the same format.
- `swagger-ui`: This folder contains the contents of the Swagger UI project. We'll need to do some minor adjustments to the `index.html` file to make it work as we expect it.

The Source Code

Here I'll list the entire code for the project, including some basic description of the code if required. I'll go folder by folder, following the order shown in Figure 7-1.

controllers

/controllers/index.js

```
module.exports = {
        BookSales: require("./booksales"),
        Stores: require("./stores"),
        Employees: require("./employees"),
        ClientReviews: require("./clientreviews"),
        Clients: require("./clients"),
        Books: require("./books"),
        Authors: require("./authors")
}
```

This file is used to export each controller. Using this technique lets us import the entire folder as if it is a module:

```
var controllers = require("/controllers")
```

/controllers/basecontroller.js

```
var _ = require("underscore"),
        restify = require("restify"),
        colors = require("colors"),
        halson = require("halson")

function BaseController() {
        this.actions = []
        this.server = null
}

BaseController.prototype.setUpActions = function(app, sw) {
        this.server = app
        _.each(this.actions, function(act) {
                var method = act['spec']['method']
                //a bit of a logging message, to help us understand what's going on
                under the hood
                console.log("Setting up auto-doc for (", method, ") - ", act['spec']
                ['nickname'])
                sw['add' + method](act)
                app[method.toLowerCase()](act['spec']['path'], act['action'])
        })
}

BaseController.prototype.addAction = function(spec, fn) {
        var newAct = {
                'spec': spec,
                action: fn
        }
        this.actions.push(newAct)
}

BaseController.prototype.RESTError = function(type, msg) {
        if(restify[type]) {
                return new restify[type](msg.toString())
        } else {
                console.log("Type " + type + " of error not found".red)
        }
}

/**
Takes care of calling the "toHAL" method on every resource before writing it
back to the client
*/
BaseController.prototype.writeHAL = function(res, obj) {
       if(Array.isArray(obj)) {
        var newArr = []
 _.each(obj, function(item, k) {
                    item = item.toHAL()
                    newArr.push(item)
               })
              obj = halson (newArr)
        } else {
```

```
        if(obj && obj.toHAL)
          obj = obj.toHAL()
        }
        if(!obj) {
          obj = {}
        }
        res.json(obj)
}

module.exports = BaseController
```

Every controller extends this object, gaining access to the methods shown earlier. We'll use basic prototypical inheritance, as you'll see in a bit when we start listing the other controllers' code.

As for this one, let's quickly go over the methods it exposes:

- `setUpActions`: This method is called upon instantiation of the controller; it is meant to add the actual routes to the HTTP server. This method is called during the initialization sequence for all controllers exported by the `index.js` file.
- `addAction`: This method defines an action, which consists of the specs for that action and the actual function code. The specs are used by Swagger to create the documentation, but they're also used by our code to set up the route; so there are bits inside the JSON spec that are also meant for the server, such as the `path` and `method` attributes.
- `RESTError`: This is a simple wrapper method around all the error methods provided by Restify.[1] It provides the benefit of cleaner code.
- `writeHAL`: Every model defined (as you'll see next) has a `toHAL` method, and the `writeHAL` methods take care of calling it for every model we're trying to render. It basically centralizes the logic that deals with collections or simple objects, depending on what we're trying to render.

■ **Tip** We're using the `colors` module here to print the error message from the `RESTError` method in red.

/controllers/books.js

```
var BaseController = require("./basecontroller"),
  _ = require("underscore"),
  swagger = require("swagger-node-restify")

function Books() {
}

Books.prototype = new BaseController()

module.exports = function(lib) {
  var controller = new Books();

  /**
    Helper function for the POST action
    */
```

[1] See `http://mcavage.me/node-restify/#error-handling`.

```
function mergeStores(list1, list2) {
  var stores1 = {}
  var stores2 = {}
  _.each(list1, function(st) {
    if(st.store)
      stores1[st.store] = st.copies
  })
  _.each(list2, function(st) {
    if(st.store)
      stores2[st.store] = st.copies
  })
  var stores = _.extend(stores1, stores2)
  return _.map(stores, function(v, k) {
    return {store: k, copies: v}
  })
}

controller.addAction({
      'path': '/books',
      'method': 'GET',
      'summary': 'Returns the list of books',
      "params": [ swagger.queryParam('q', 'Search term', 'string'), swagger.
      queryParam('genre','Filter by genre', 'string')],
      'responseClass': 'Book',
      'nickname': 'getBooks'
    }, function(req, res, next) {

      var criteria = {}
      if(req.params.q) {
        var expr = new RegExp('.*' + req.params.q + '.*')
        criteria.$or = [
          {title: expr},
          {isbn_code: expr},
          {description: expr}
        ]
      }
      if(req.params.genre) {
        criteria.genre = req.params.genre
      }

      lib.db.model('Book')
        .find(criteria)
        .populate('stores.store')
        .exec(function(err, books) {
        if(err) return next(err)
        controller.writeHAL(res, books)
      })
    })

 controller.addAction({
      'path': '/books/{id}',
      'method': 'GET',
      'params': [ swagger.pathParam('id', 'The Id of the book','int') ],
```

```
      'summary': 'Returns the full data of a book',
      'nickname': 'getBook'
    }, function(req, res, next) {
      var id = req.params.id
      if(id) {
        lib.db.model("Book")
          .findOne({_id: id})
          .populate('authors')
          .populate('stores')
          .populate('reviews')
          .exec(function(err, book) {
            if(err) return next(controller.RESTError('InternalServerError', err))
            if(!book) {
              return next(controller.RESTError('ResourceNotFoundError', 'Book not
              found'))
            }

            controller.writeHAL(res, book)
          })

      } else {
        next(controller.RESTError('InvalidArgumentError', 'Missing book id'))
      }
    })

  controller.addAction({
      'path': '/books',
      'method': 'POST',
      'params': [ swagger.bodyParam('book', 'JSON representation of the new
      book','string') ],
      'summary': 'Adds a new book into the collectoin',
      'nickname': 'newBook'
    }, function(req, res, next) {
      var bookData = req.body
      if(bookData) {
        isbn = bookData.isbn_code
        lib.db.model("Book")
          .findOne({isbn_code: isbn})
          .exec(function(err, bookModel) {
            if(!bookModel) {
              bookModel = lib.db.model("Book")(bookData)
            } else {
              bookModel.stores = mergeStores(bookModel.stores, bookData.stores)
            }
            bookModel.save(function(err, book) {
                if(err) return next(controller.RESTError('InternalServerError', err))
                controller.writeHAL(res, book)
              })
          })
      } else {
        next(controller.RESTError('InvalidArgumentError', 'Missing content of book'))
      }
    })
```

```
controller.addAction({
      'path': '/books/{id}/authors',
      'method': 'GET',
      'params': [ swagger.pathParam('id', 'The Id of the book','int') ],
      'summary': 'Returns the list of authors of one specific book',
      'nickname': 'getBooksAuthors'
    }, function(req, res, next) {
      var id = req.params.id
      if(id) {
        lib.db.model("Book")
          .findOne({_id: id})
          .populate('authors')
          .exec(function(err, book) {
            if(err) return next(controller.RESTError('InternalServerError', err))
            if(!book) {
              return next(controller.RESTError('ResourceNotFoundError', 'Book not
              found'))
            }
            controller.writeHAL(res, book.authors)
          })
      } else {
        next(controller.RESTError('InvalidArgumentError', 'Missing book id'))
      }
    })

controller.addAction({
      'path': '/books/{id}/reviews',
      'method': 'GET',
      'params': [ swagger.pathParam('id', 'The Id of the book','int') ],
      'summary': 'Returns the list of reviews of one specific book',
      'nickname': 'getBooksReviews'
    }, function(req, res,next) {
      var id = req.params.id
      if(id) {
        lib.db.model("Book")
          .findOne({_id: id})
          .populate('reviews')
          .exec(function(err, book) {
            if(err) return next(controller.RESTError('InternalServerError', err))
            if(!book) {
              return next(controller.RESTError('ResourceNotFoundError', 'Book not
              found'))
            }
            controller.writeHAL(res, book.reviews)
          })
      } else {
        next(controller.RESTError('InvalidArgumentError', 'Missing book id'))
      }
    })

controller.addAction({
      'path': '/books/{id}',
      'method': 'PUT',
```

```
            'params': [ swagger.pathParam('id', 'The Id of the book to update','string'),
                        swagger.bodyParam('book', 'The data to change on the book',
                        'string') ],
            'summary': 'Updates the information of one specific book',
            'nickname': 'updateBook'
        }, function(req, res, next) {
            var data = req.body
            var id = req.params.id
            if(id) {

              lib.db.model("Book").findOne({_id: id}).exec(function(err, book) {
              if(err) return next(controller.RESTError('InternalServerError', err))
                if(!book) return next(controller.RESTError('ResourceNotFoundError',
                'Book not found'))
                book = _.extend(book, data)
                book.save(function(err, data) {
                if(err) return next(controller.RESTError('InternalServerError', err))
                 controller.writeHAL(res, data.toJSON())
                })
              })
            } else {
              next(controller.RESTError('InvalidArgumentError', 'Invalid id received'))
            }
        })
      return controller
    }
```

The code for this controller is very straightforward; in it are the basic mechanics defined for this particular project on how to declare a controller and its actions. We also have a special case for the POST action, which checks the ISBN of a new book to see if it is in stock at another store. If an ISBN already exists, the book is merged to all relevant stores; otherwise, a new record is created.

In theory, we're creating a new function that inherits from the `BaseController`, which gives us the ability to add custom behavior on a specific controller. Reality is going to prove that we don't really need such liberties, however. And we could very well do the same by instantiating the `BaseController` directly on every other controller file.

The controller files are required during initialization of the API, and when that happens, the `lib` object is passed to them, like so:

```
var controller = require("/controllers/books.js")(lib)
```

This means that (as you see in the preceding code), the `lib` object is received by the export function, which is in charge of instantiating the new controller and adding actions to it to return it to the required code.

Here are some other interesting bits from the code:

- The `getBooks` action shows how to do simple regular expression-based filtering with Mongoose.
- The `update` action is not actually using the `update` method from Mongoose, but instead loads the model using the `extend` method from the underscore, and finally calls the `save` method on the model. This is done for one simple reason: the `update` method doesn't trigger any post hooks on the models, but the `save` method does, so if we wanted to add behavior to react to an update on the model, this would be the way to go about it.

/controllers/stores.js

```
var BaseController = require("./basecontroller"),
        _ = require("underscore"),
        swagger = require("swagger-node-restify")

function Stores() {
}

Stores.prototype = new BaseController()

module.exports = function(lib) {
  var controller = new Stores();

  controller.addAction({
        'path': '/stores',
        'method': 'GET',
        'summary': 'Returns the list of stores ',
    'params': [swagger.queryParam('state', 'Filter the list of stores by state',
    'string')],
        'responseClass': 'Store',
        'nickname': 'getStores'
  }, function (req, res, next) {
    var criteria = {}
    if(req.params.state) {
      criteria.state = new RegExp(req.params.state,'i')
    }
        lib.db.model('Store')
      .find(criteria)
      .exec(function(err, list) {
                if(err) return next(controller.RESTError('InternalServerError', err))
      controller.writeHAL(res, list)
        })
  })

  controller.addAction({
        'path': '/stores/{id}',
        'method': 'GET',
        'params': [swagger.pathParam('id','The id of the store','string')],
        'summary': 'Returns the data of a store',
        'responseClass': 'Store',
        'nickname': 'getStore'
  }, function(req, res, next) {
    var id = req.params.id
    if(id) {
      lib.db.model('Store')
        .findOne({_id: id})
        .populate('employees')
        .exec(function(err, data) {
        if(err) return next(controller.RESTError('InternalServerError', err))
        if(!data) return next(controller.RESTError('ResourceNotFoundError', 'Store
        not found'))

        controller.writeHAL(res, data)
      })
```

```
    } else {
      next(controller.RESTError('InvalidArgumentError', 'Invalid id'))
    }
  })

  controller.addAction({
    'path': '/stores/{id}/books',
    'method': 'GET',
    'params': [swagger.pathParam('id','The id of the store','string'),
               swagger.queryParam('q', 'Search parameter for the books', 'string'),
               swagger.queryParam('genre', 'Filter results by genre', 'string')],
    'summary': 'Returns the list of books of a store',
    'responseClass': 'Book',
    'nickname': 'getStoresBooks'
  }, function (req, res, next) {
    var id = req.params.id
    if(id) {

      var criteria = {stores: id}
      if(req.params.q) {
        var expr = new RegExp('.*' + req.params.q + '.*', 'i')
        criteria.$or = [
          {title: expr},
          {isbn_code: expr},
          {description: expr}
        ]
      }
      if(req.params.genre) {
        criteria.genre = req.params.genre
      }

      //even though this is the stores controller, we deal directly with books here
      lib.db.model('Book')
        .find(criteria)
        .populate('authors')
        .exec(function(err, data) {
          if(err) return next(controller.RESTError('InternalServerError', err))
          controller.writeHAL(res, data)
        })
    } else {
      next(controller.RESTError('InvalidArgumentError', 'Invalid id'))
    }
  })

  controller.addAction({
    'path': '/stores/{id}/employees',
    'method': 'GET',
    'params': [swagger.pathParam('id','The id of the store','string')],
    'summary': 'Returns the list of employees working on a store',
    'responseClass': 'Employee',
    'nickname': 'getStoresEmployees'
  }, function (req, res, next) {
    var id = req.params.id
```

```
  if(id) {
    lib.db.model('Store')
      .findOne({_id: id})
      .populate('employees')
      .exec(function(err, data) {
        if(err) return next(controller.RESTError('InternalServerError', err))
        if(!data) {
          return next(controller.RESTError('ResourceNotFoundError', 'Store not
          found'))
        }
        console.log(data)
        controller.writeHAL(res, data.employees)
      })
  } else  {
    next(controller.RESTError('InvalidArgumentError', 'Invalid id'))
  }
})

controller.addAction({
  'path': '/stores/{id}/booksales',
  'method': 'GET',
  'params': [swagger.pathParam('id','The id of the store','string')],
  'summary': 'Returns the list of booksales done on a store',
  'responseClass': 'BookSale',
  'nickname': 'getStoresBookSales'
}, function (req, res, next) {
  var id = req.params.id
  if(id) {
    //even though this is the stores controller, we deal directly with booksales here
    lib.db.model('Booksale')
      .find({store: id})
      .populate('client')
      .populate('employee')
      .populate('books')
      .exec(function(err, data) {
        if(err) return next(controller.RESTError('InternalServerError', err))
        controller.writeHAL(res, data)
      })
  } else  {
    next(controller.RESTError('InvalidArgumentError', 'Invalid id'))
  }
})

controller.addAction({
      'path': '/stores',
      'method': 'POST',
      'summary': 'Adds a new store to the list',
  'params': [swagger.bodyParam('store', 'The JSON data of the store', 'string')],
      'responseClass': 'Store',
      'nickname': 'newStore'
}, function (req, res, next) {
      var data = req.body
```

```
        if(data) {
                var newStore = lib.db.model('Store')(data)
                newStore.save(function(err, store) {
                          if(err) return next(controller.RESTError('InternalServerErr
                          or', err))
                        res.json(controller.toHAL(store))
                })
        } else {
                next(controller.RESTError('InvalidArgumentError', 'No data
received'))
        }
  })

  controller.addAction({
        'path': '/stores/{id}',
        'method': 'PUT',
        'summary': "UPDATES a store's information",
        'params': [swagger.pathParam('id','The id of the store','string'), swagger.
        bodyParam('store', 'The new information to update', 'string')],
        'responseClass': 'Store',
        'nickname': 'updateStore'
  }, function (req, res, next) {
        var data = req.body
        var id = req.params.id
        if(id) {
                lib.db.model("Store").findOne({_id: id}).exec(function(err, store) {
                        if(err) return next(controller.RESTError('InternalServerErr
                        or', err))
        if(!store) return next(controller.RESTError('ResourceNotFoundError', 'Store
        not found'))
                        store = _.extend(store, data)
                        store.save(function(err, data) {
                                if(err) return next(controller.RESTError('InternalSer
                                verError', err))
                                 res.json(controller.toHAL(data))
                        })
                })
        } else {
                next(controller.RESTError('InvalidArgumentError', 'Invalid id
                received'))
        }
  })

  return controller
}
```

The code for the Stores controller is very similar to that of the Books controller. It does, however, have something of notice: the `getStoresBookSales` action clearly shows what happens when we don't use a Hierarchical MVC model. I said that this is not a common case, so it would be fine for the purpose of this book, but it shows how separation of concerns is broken in the strictest of senses by acting over the model of another controller, instead of going through that other controller. Given the added complexity that mechanism would imply to our code, we're better off looking the other way for the time being.

Here are the remaining controllers. They don't particularly show anything new compared to the previous ones, so just look at the code and the occasional code comment.

/controllers/authors.js

```
var BaseController = require("./basecontroller"),
  swagger = require("swagger-node-restify")
function BookSales() {

}

BookSales.prototype = new BaseController()

module.exports = function(lib) {
  var controller = new BookSales()

  //list
  controller.addAction({
        'path': '/authors',
        'method': 'GET',
        'summary' :'Returns the list of authors across all stores',
        'params': [ swagger.queryParam('genre', 'Filter authors by genre of their
        books', 'string'),
                                swagger.queryParam('q', 'Search parameter', 'string')],
        'responseClass': 'Author',
        'nickname': 'getAuthors'
  }, function(req, res, next) {

        var criteria = {}
    if(req.params.q) {
      var expr = new RegExp('.*' + req.params.q + '.*', 'i')
      criteria.$or = [
        {name: expr},
        {description: expr}
      ]
    }
    var filterByGenre = false || req.params.genre

    if(filterByGenre) {
        lib.db.model('Book')
                .find({genre: filterByGenre})
                .exec(function(err, books) {
                        if(err) return next(controller.RESTError('InternalServerErr
                        or', err))
                        findAuthors(_.pluck(books, '_id'))
                })
    } else {
        findAuthors()
    }

    function findAuthors(bookIds) {
        if(bookIds) {
                criteria.books = {$in: bookIds}
        }
```

```
                lib.db.model('Author')
                        .find(criteria)
                        .exec(function(err, authors) {
                                if(err) return next(controller.RESTError('InternalSer
                                verError', err))
                                controller.writeHAL(res, authors)
                        })
    }

})
//get
controller.addAction({
        'path': '/authors/{id}',
        'summary': 'Returns all the data from one specific author',
        'method': 'GET',
        'responseClass': 'Author',
        'nickname': 'getAuthor'
}, function (req, res, next) {
        var id = req.params.id

        if(id) {
                lib.db.model('Author')
                        .findOne({_id: id})
                        .exec(function(err, author) {
                                if(err) return next(controller.RESTError('InternalSer
                                verError', err))
                                if(!author) {
                                        return next(controller.RESTError('ResourceNot
                                        FoundError', 'Author not found'))
                                }
                                controller.writeHAL(res, author)
                        })
        } else {
              next(controller.RESTError('InvalidArgumentError', 'Missing author id'))
        }
})

//post

controller.addAction({
        'path': '/authors',
        'summary': 'Adds a new author to the database',
        'method': 'POST',
        'params': [swagger.bodyParam('author', 'JSON representation of the data',
        'string')],
        'responseClass': 'Author',
        'nickname': 'addAuthor'
}, function (req, res, next) {
        var body = req.body

        if(body) {
                var newAuthor = lib.db.model('Author')(body)
                newAuthor.save(function(err, author) {
                 if(err) return next(controller.RESTError('InternalServerError', err))
```

```
                    controller.writeHAL(res, author)
                })
        } else {
                next(controller.RESTError('InvalidArgumentError', 'Missing author id'))
        }
})
  //put

  controller.addAction({
        'path': '/authors/{id}',
        'method': 'PUT',
        'summary': "UPDATES an author's information",
        'params': [swagger.pathParam('id','The id of the author','string'),
                        swagger.bodyParam('author', 'The new information to
                        update', 'string')],
        'responseClass': 'Author',
        'nickname': 'updateAuthor'
  }, function (req, res, next) {
        var data = req.body
        var id = req.params.id
        if(id) {

                lib.db.model("Author").findOne({_id: id}).exec(function(err, author) {
                 if(err) return next(controller.RESTError('InternalServerError', err))
                 if(!author) return next(controller.RESTError('ResourceNotFoundError',
                 'Author not found'))
                        author = _.extend(author, data)
                        author.save(function(err, data) {
                                if(err) return next(controller.RESTError('Int
                                ernalServerError', err))
                                res.json(controller.toHAL(data))
                        })
                })
        } else {
                next(controller.RESTError('InvalidArgumentError', 'Invalid id
                received'))
        }
  })

  // /books
  controller.addAction({
        'path': '/authors/{id}/books',
        'summary': 'Returns the data from all the books of one specific author',
        'method': 'GET',
        'params': [ swagger.pathParam('id', 'The id of the author', 'string')],
        'responseClass': 'Book',
        'nickname': 'getAuthorsBooks'
  }, function (req, res, next) {
        var id = req.params.id

        if(id) {
                lib.db.model('Author')
                        .findOne({_id: id})
```

```
                         .populate('books')
                         .exec(function(err, author) {
                                 if(err) return next(controller.RESTError('InternalSer
                                 verError', err))
                                 if(!author) {
                                         return next(controller.RESTError('ResourceNot
                                         FoundError', 'Author not found'))
                                 }
                                 controller.writeHAL(res, author.books)
                         })
         } else {
              next(controller.RESTError('InvalidArgumentError', 'Missing author id'))
         }
  })

  return controller
}
```

/controllers/booksales.js

```
var BaseController = require("./basecontroller"),
  swagger = require("swagger-node-restify")

function BookSales() {

}

BookSales.prototype = new BaseController()

module.exports = function(lib) {
  var controller = new BookSales();

  controller.addAction({
        'path': '/booksales',
        'method': 'GET',
        'summary': 'Returns the list of book sales',
        'params': [ swagger.queryParam('start_date', 'Filter sales done after (or on)
                    this date', 'string'),
                    swagger.queryParam('end_date', 'Filter sales done on or before
                    this date', 'string'),
                    swagger.queryParam('store_id', 'Filter sales done  on this
                    store', 'string')
                  ],
        'responseClass': 'BookSale',
        'nickname': 'getBookSales'
      }, function(req, res, next) {
        console.log(req)

        var criteria = {}
        if(req.params.start_date)
          criteria.date = {$gte: req.params.start_date}
        if(req.params.end_date)
          criteria.date = {$lte: req.params.end_date}
```

```
        if(req.params.store_id)
          criteria.store = req.params.store_id

        lib.db.model("Booksale")
          .find(criteria)
          .populate('books')
          .populate('client')
          .populate('employee')
          .populate('store')
          .exec(function(err, sales) {
          if(err) return next(controller.RESTError('InternalServerError', err))
          controller.writeHAL(res, sales)
        })
      })

  controller.addAction({
        'path': '/booksales',
        'method': 'POST',
        'params': [ swagger.bodyParam('booksale', 'JSON representation of the new
        booksale','string') ],
        'summary': 'Records a new booksale',
        'nickname': 'newBookSale'
      }, function(req, res, next) {
        var body = req.body
        if(body) {
          var newSale = lib.db.model("Booksale")(body)
          newSale.save(function(err, sale) {
            if(err) return next(controller.RESTError('InternalServerError', err))
            controller.writeHAL(res, sale)
          })
        } else {
          next(controller.RESTError('InvalidArgumentError', 'Missing json data'))
        }
      })

  return controller
}
```

/controllers/clientreviews.js

```
var BaseController = require("./basecontroller"),
        _ = require("underscore"),
        swagger = require("swagger-node-restify")

function ClientReviews() {
}

ClientReviews.prototype = new BaseController()

module.exports = function(lib) {
  var controller = new ClientReviews();

  controller.addAction({
        'path': '/clientreviews',
```

```
            'method': 'POST',
            'summary': 'Adds a new client review to a book',
            'params': [swagger.bodyParam('review', 'The JSON representation of the
            review',  'string')],
            'responseClass': 'ClientReview',
            'nickname': 'addClientReview'
      }, function (req, res, next) {
            var body = req.body
            if(body) {

                    var newReview = lib.db.model('ClientReview')(body)
                    newReview.save(function (err, rev) {
                      if(err) return next(controller.RESTError('InternalServerError', err))
                           controller.writeHAL(res, rev)
                    })
            }
      })

      return controller
    }
```

/controllers/clients.js

```
    var BaseController = require("./basecontroller"),
            _ = require("underscore"),
            swagger = require("swagger-node-restify")

    function Clients() {
    }

    Clients.prototype = new BaseController()

    module.exports = function(lib) {
      var controller = new Clients();

      controller.addAction({
            'path': '/clients',
            'method': 'GET',
            'summary': 'Returns the list of clients ordered by name',
            'responsClass':'Client',
            'nickname': 'getClients'
      }, function(req, res, next) {
            lib.db.model('Client').find().sort('name').exec(function(err, clients) {
                    if(err) return next(controller.RESTError('InternalServerError', err))
          controller.writeHAL(res, clients)
            })
      })

      controller.addAction({
            'path': '/clients',
            'method': 'POST',
            'params': [swagger.bodyParam('client', 'The JSON representation of the
            client', 'string')],
            'summary': 'Adds a new client to the database',
```

```
        'responsClass': 'Client',
        'nickname': 'addClient'
  }, function(req, res, next) {
        var newClient = req.body

        var newClientModel = lib.db.model('Client')(newClient)
        newClientModel.save(function(err, client) {
                if(err) return next(controller.RESTError('InternalServerError', err))
      controller.writeHAL(res, client)
        })
  })

  controller.addAction({
        'path': '/clients/{id}',
        'method': 'GET',
        'params': [swagger.pathParam('id', 'The id of the client', 'string')],
        'summary': 'Returns the data of one client',
        'responsClass': 'Client',
        'nickname': 'getClient'
  }, function (req, res, next) {
        var id = req.params.id
        if(id != null) {
                lib.db.model('Client').findOne({_id: id}).exec(function(err, client){
                   if(err) return next(controller.RESTError('InternalServerError',err))
        if(!client) return next(controller.RESTError('ResourceNotFoundError', 'The
        client id cannot be found'))
          controller.writeHAL(res, client)
                })
        } else {
              next(controller.RESTError('InvalidArgumentError','Invalid client id'))
        }
  })

  controller.addAction({
        'path': '/clients/{id}',
        'method': 'PUT',
        'params': [swagger.pathParam('id', 'The id of the client', 'string'),
swagger.bodyParam('client', 'The content to overwrite', 'string')],
        'summary': 'Updates the data of one client',
        'responsClass': 'Client',
        'nickname': 'updateClient'
  }, function (req, res, next) {
        var id = req.params.id
        if(!id) {
                return next(controller.RESTError('InvalidArgumentError','Invalid id'))
        } else {
                var model = lib.db.model('Client')
                model.findOne({_id: id})
                        .exec(function(err, client) {
                              if(err) return next(controller.RESTError('InternalServe
                              rError', err))
                                client = _.extend(client, req.body)
                                client.save(function(err, newClient) {
```

```
                                                    if(err) return next(controller.RESTError('Int
                                                    ernalServerError', err))
                        controller.writeHAL(res, newClient)
                                            })
                                    })
                    }
        })

        return controller
}
```

/controllers/employees.js

```
var BaseController = require("./basecontroller"),
        _ = require("underscore"),
        swagger = require("swagger-node-restify")

function Employees() {
}

Employees.prototype = new BaseController()

module.exports = function(lib) {
  var controller = new Employees();

  controller.addAction({
        'path': '/employees',
        'method': 'GET',
        'summary': 'Returns the list of employees across all stores',
        'responseClass': 'Employee',
        'nickname': 'getEmployees'
  }, function(req, res, next) {
        lib.db.model('Employee').find().exec(function(err, list) {
                if(err) return next(controller.RESTError('InternalServerError', err))
            controller.writeHAL(res, list)
        })
  })

  controller.addAction({
        'path': '/employees/{id}',
        'method': 'GET',
        'params': [swagger.pathParam('id','The id of the employee','string')],
        'summary': 'Returns the data of an employee',
        'responseClass': 'Employee',
        'nickname': 'getEmployee'
  }, function(req, res, next) {
        var id = req.params.id
        if(id) {
                lib.db.model('Employee').findOne({_id: id}).exec(function(err, empl) {
                        if(err) return next(err)
                        if(!empl) {
                                return next(controller.RESTError('ResourceNotFoundErr
                                or', 'Not found'))
                        }
```

```
            controller.writeHAL(res, empl)
                    })
                    } else  {
                        next(controller.RESTError('InvalidArgumentError', 'Invalid id'))
                }
    })

    controller.addAction({
            'path': '/employees',
            'method': 'POST',
            'params': [swagger.bodyParam('employee', 'The JSON data of the employee',
            'string')],
            'summary': 'Adds a new employee to the list',
            'responseClass': 'Employee',
            'nickname': 'newEmployee'
    }, function(req, res, next) {
            var data = req.body
            if(data) {
                    var newEmployee = lib.db.model('Employee')(data)
                    newEmployee.save(function(err, emp) {
                                    if(err) return next(controller.RESTError('InternalSer
                                    verError', err))
                            controller.writeHAL(res, emp)
                    })
            } else {
                    next(controller.RESTError('InvalidArgumentError', 'No data received'))
            }
    })

    controller.addAction({
            'path': '/employees/{id}',
            'method': 'PUT',
            'summary': "UPDATES an employee's information",
            'params': [swagger.pathParam('id','The id of the employee','string'),
swagger.bodyParam('employee', 'The new information to update', 'string')],
            'responseClass': 'Employee',
            'nickname': 'updateEmployee'
    }, function(req, res, next) {
            var data = req.body
            var id = req.params.id
            if(id) {

                    lib.db.model("Employee").findOne({_id: id}).exec(function(err, emp) {
                                    if(err) return next(controller.RESTError('InternalSer
                                    verError', err))
                            emp = _.extend(emp, data)
                            emp.save(function(err, employee) {
                                            if(err) return next(controller.RESTError('Int
                                            ernalServerError', err))
                                            controller.writeHAL(res, employee)
                            })
                    })
            } else {
```

```
                next(controller.RESTError('InvalidArgumentError','Invalid id
                received'))
            }
    })

    return controller
}
```

lib

As mentioned, the lib folder contains all sorts of helper functions and utilities that were just too small to be put into a separate folder, but important and generic enough to be used in several places of the code.

/lib/index.js

```
var lib = {
        helpers: require("./helpers"),
        config: require("./config"),
        controllers: require("../controllers"),
        schemas: require("../schemas"),
        schemaValidator: require("./schemaValidator"),
        db: require("./db")
}

module.exports = lib
```

This file is supposed to act as the single point of contact between the outside world (the rest of the project) and the inside world (all of the mini-modules grouped within this folder). There is nothing special about it. It just requires everything and exports using predefined keys.

/lib/helpers.js

```
var halson = require("halson"),
        _ = require("underscore")

module.exports = {
        makeHAL: makeHAL,
        setupRoutes: setupRoutes,
        validateKey: validateKey
}

function setupRoutes(server, swagger, lib) {
        for(controller in lib.controllers) {
                cont = lib.controllers[controller](lib)
                cont.setUpActions(server, swagger)
        }
}
/**
Makes sure to sign every request and compare it
against the key sent by the client, this way
we make sure its authentic
```

```
*/
function validateKey(hmacdata, key, lib) {
        //This is for testing the swagger-ui, should be removed after development to
        avoid possible security problem :)
        if(+key == 777) return true
        var hmac = require("crypto").createHmac("md5", lib.config.secretKey)
          .update(hmacdata)
          .digest("hex");
        //TODO: Remove this line
        console.log(hmac)
        return hmac == key
}

function makeHAL(data, links, embed) {
        var obj = halson(data)

        if(links && links.length > 0) {
                _.each(links, function(lnk) {
                        obj.addLink(lnk.name, {
                                href: lnk.href,
                                title: lnk.title || ''
                        })
                })
        }
        if(embed && embed.length > 0) {
                _.each(embed, function (item) {
                        obj.addEmbed(item.name, item.data)
                })
        }

        return obj
}
```

Just as the modules exported by the index.js file are too small to merit their own folder, these functions are too small and particular to merit their own module, so instead they are grouped here, inside the helpers module. The functions are meant to be of use (hence, the name "helpers") throughout the entire project.

Let's quickly go over each of these names:

> setupRoutes: This function is called from within the project's main file during boot-up time. It's meant to initialize all controllers, which in turn adds the actual route's code to the HTTP server.
>
> validateKey: This function contains the code to validate the request by recalculating the HMAC key. And as mentioned earlier, it contains the exception to the rule, allowing any request to validate if the key sent is 777.
>
> makeHAL: This function turns any type of object into a HAL JSON object ready to be rendered. This particular function is heavily used from within the models' code.

/lib/schemaValidator.js

```
var tv4 = require("tv4"),
        formats = require("tv4-formats"),
```

```
        schemas = require("../request_schemas/")

module.exports = {
        validateRequest: validate
}

function validate (req) {
        var res = {valid: true}
        tv4.addFormat(formats)
        var schemaKey = req.route ? req.route.path.toString().replace("/", "") : ''
        var actionKey = req.route.name
        if(schemas[schemaKey])      {
                var mySchema = schemas[schemaKey][actionKey]
                var data = null
                if(mySchema) {
                        switch(mySchema.validate) {
                                case 'params':
                                        data = req.params
                                break
                        }
                        res = tv4.validateMultiple(data, mySchema.schema)
                }
        }

        return res
}
```

This file has the code that validates any request against a JSON Schema that we define. The only function of interest is the `validate` function, which validates the request object. It also counts on a predefined structure inside the request, which is added by Swagger (the `route` attribute).

As you might've guessed from the preceding code, the validation of a request is optional; not every request is being validated. And right now, only query parameters are validated, but this can be extended by simply adding a new case to the switch statement.

This function works with the premise of "convention over configuration," which means that if you set up everything "right," then you don't have to do much. In our particular case, we're looking inside the `request_schemas` folder to load a set of predefined schemas, which have a very specific format. In that format we find the name of the action (the nickname that we set up) to validate and the portion of the request we want to validate. In our particular function, we're only validating query parameters for things such as invalid formats and so forth. The only request we have set up to validate right now is the BookSales listing action; but if we wanted to add a new validation, it would just be a matter of adding a new schema—no programming required.

/lib/db.js

```
var config = require("./config"),
        _ = require("underscore"),
        mongoose = require("mongoose"),

        Schema = mongoose.Schema

var obj = {
        cachedModels: {},
        getModelFromSchema: getModelFromSchema,
        model: function(mname) {
```

```
                return this.models[mname]
        },
        connect: function(cb) {
                mongoose.connect(config.database.host + "/" + config.database.dbname)
                this.connection = mongoose.connection
                this.connection.on('error', cb)
                this.connection.on('open', cb)
        }
}

obj.models = require("../models/")(obj)

module.exports = obj

function translateComplexType(v, strType) {
        var tmp = null
        var type = strType || v['type']
        switch(type) {
                case 'array':
                        tmp = []
                        if(v['items']['$ref'] != null) {
                                tmp.push({
                                        type: Schema.ObjectId,
                                        ref: v['items']['$ref']
                                })
                        } else {
                                var originalType = v['items']['type']
                                v['items']['type'] = translateTypeToJs(v['items']
                                ['type'])
                                tmp.push(translateComplexType(v['items'],
                                originalType))
                        }
                break;
                case 'object':
                        tmp = {}
                        var props = v['properties']
                        _.each(props, function(data, k) {
                                if(data['$ref'] != null) {
                                        tmp[k] = {
                                                type: Schema.ObjectId,
                                                ref: data['$ref']
                                        }
                                } else {
                                        tmp[k] = translateTypeToJs(data['type'])
                                }
                        })
                break;
                default:
                        tmp = v
                        tmp['type'] = translateTypeToJs(type)
                break;
        }
```

```
        return tmp
}

/**
Turns the JSON Schema into a Mongoose schema
*/
function getModelFromSchema(schema) {
        var data = {
                name: schema.id,
                schema: {}
        }

        var newSchema = {}
        var tmp = null
        _.each(schema.properties, function(v, propName) {
                if(v['$ref'] != null) {
                        tmp = {
                                type: Schema.ObjectId,
                                ref: v['$ref']
                        }
                } else {
                        tmp = translateComplexType(v) //{}
                }
                newSchema[propName] = tmp
        })
        data.schema = new Schema(newSchema)
        return data
}

function translateTypeToJs(t) {
        if(t.indexOf('int') === 0) {
                t = "number"
        }
        return eval(t.charAt(0).toUpperCase() + t.substr(1))
}
```

This file contains some interesting functions that are used a lot from the models' code. In Chapter 5 I mentioned that the schemas used with Swagger could potentially be reused to do other things, such as defining the models' schemas. But to do this, we need a function to translate the standard JSON Schema into the nonstandard JSON format required by Mongoose to define a model. This is where the `getModelFromSchema` function comes into play; its code is meant to go over the structure of the JSON Schema and create a new, simpler JSON structure to be used as a Mongoose Schema.

The other functions are more straightforward:

- *connect:* Connects to the database server and sets up the callbacks for both error and success cases.
- *model:* Accesses the model from outside. We could just directly access the models using the object *models,* but it's always a good idea to provide a wrapper in case you ever need to add extra behaviors (such as checking for errors).

/lib/config.js

```
module.exports = {
	secretKey: 'this is a secret key, right here',
	server: {
		name: 'ComeNRead API',
		version: '1.0.0',
		port: 9000
	},
	database: {
		host: 'mongodb://localhost',
		dbname: 'comenread'
	}
}
```

This file is very straightforward; it simply exports a set of constant values to be used throughout the entire application.

models

This folder contains the actual code of each model. The definition of these resources won't be found in these files because they're only meant to define behavior. The actual properties are defined in the schemas folder (which, again, is being used both by the models and Swagger).

/models/index.js

```
module.exports = function(db) {
	return {
		"Book": require("./book")(db),
		"Booksale": require("./booksale")(db),
		"ClientReview": require("./clientreview")(db),
		"Client": require("./client")(db),
		"Employee": require("./employee")(db),
		"Store": require("./store")(db),
		"Author": require("./author")(db)
	}
}
```

Again, as in the other folders, the index.js file allows us to require every model at once, and treat this folder like a module itself. The other thing of note here is the passing of the db object to every model, so that they can access the getModelFromSchema function.

/models/author.js

```
var mongoose = require("mongoose")
	jsonSelect = require('mongoose-json-select'),
	helpers = require("../lib/helpers"),
	_ = require("underscore")
```

```
module.exports = function(db) {
        var schema = require("../schemas/author.js")
        var modelDef = db.getModelFromSchema(schema)

        modelDef.schema.plugin(jsonSelect, '-books')
        modelDef.schema.methods.toHAL = function() {
                var halObj = helpers.makeHAL(this.toJSON(),
                        [{name: 'books', 'href': '/authors/' + this.id + '/books',
                        'title': 'Books'}])

                if(this.books.length > 0) {
                        if(this.books[0].toString().length != 24) {
                                halObj.addEmbed('books', _.map(this.books,
                                function(e) { return e.toHAL() }))

                        }
                }

                return halObj
        }

        return mongoose.model(modelDef.name, modelDef.schema)
}
```

The code of the Author model shows the basic mechanics of loading the JSON Schema, transforming it into a Mongoose Schema, defining the custom behavior, and finally returning a new model.

The following defines the main custom behaviors:

- The `jsonSelect` model allows us to define the attributes to add to or remove from the object when turning it into a JSON. We want to remove the embedded objects from the JSON representation, because they will be added to the HAL JSON representation as embedded objects, rather than being part of the main object.
- The `toHAL` method takes care of returning the representation of the resource in JSON HAL format.
- The links associated to the main object are defined manually. We could improve this by further customizing the code for the loading and transformation of the JSON Schemas of the models.

▒ **Note** Checks like the following (inside the `toHAL` method) are meant to determine if the model has populated a reference, or if it is simply the id of the referenced object:

```
if(this.books[0].toString().length != 24) {
  //...
}
```

The following is the rest of the code inside the *models* folder, as you can appreciate, the same mechanics are duplicated on every case.

/models/book.js

```
var mongoose = require("mongoose"),
        jsonSelect = require('mongoose-json-select'),
        helpers = require("../lib/helpers"),
        _ = require("underscore")

module.exports = function(db) {
        var schema = require("../schemas/book.js")
        var modelDef = db.getModelFromSchema(schema)

        modelDef.schema.plugin(jsonSelect, '-stores -authors')
        modelDef.schema.methods.toHAL = function() {
                var halObj = helpers.makeHAL(this.toJSON(),
                     [{name: 'reviews', href: '/books/' + this.id + '/reviews',
                     title: 'Reviews'}])

                if(this.stores.length > 0) {
                        if(this.stores[0].store.toString().length != 24) {
                     halObj.addEmbed('stores', _.map(this.stores, function(s) {
                     return { store: s.store.toHAL(), copies: s.copies } } ))
                        }
                }

                if(this.authors.length > 0) {
                        if(this.authors[0].toString().length != 24) {
                                halObj.addEmbed('authors', this.authors)
                        }
                }

                return halObj
        }

        return mongoose.model(modelDef.name, modelDef.schema)
}
```

/models/booksale.js

```
var mongoose = require("mongoose"),
        jsonSelect = require('mongoose-json-select'),
        helpers = require("../lib/helpers"),
        _ = require("underscore")
module.exports = function(db) {
        var schema = require("../schemas/booksale.js")
        var modelDef = db.getModelFromSchema(schema)

        modelDef.schema.plugin(jsonSelect, '-store -employee -client -books')
        modelDef.schema.methods.toHAL = function() {
                var halObj = helpers.makeHAL(this.toJSON())

                if(this.books.length > 0) {
                        if(this.books[0].toString().length != 24) {
                                halObj.addEmbed('books', _.map(this.books,
                                function(b) { return b.toHAL() }))
                        }
                }
```

```
                if(this.store.toString().length != 24) {
                        halObj.addEmbed('store', this.store.toHAL())
                }
                if(this.employee.toString().length != 24) {
                        halObj.addEmbed('employee', this.employee.toHAL())
                }
                if(this.client.toString().length != 24) {
                        halObj.addEmbed('client', this.client.toHAL())
                }
                return halObj
        }
        return mongoose.model(modelDef.name, modelDef.schema)
}
```

/models/client.js

```
var mongoose = require("mongoose"),
        jsonSelect = require('mongoose-json-select'),
        helpers = require("../lib/helpers"),
        _ = require("underscore")
module.exports = function(db) {
        var schema = require("../schemas/client.js")
        var modelDef = db.getModelFromSchema(schema)
        modelDef.schema.methods.toHAL = function() {
                var halObj = helpers.makeHAL(this.toJSON())
                return halObj
        }
        return mongoose.model(modelDef.name, modelDef.schema)
}
```

/models/clientreview.js

```
var mongoose = require("mongoose"),
        jsonSelect = require('mongoose-json-select'),
        helpers = require("../lib/helpers"),
        _ = require("underscore")
module.exports = function(db) {
        var schema = require("../schemas/clientreview.js")
        var modelDef = db.getModelFromSchema(schema)
        modelDef.schema.methods.toHAL = function() {
                var halObj = helpers.makeHAL(this.toJSON())
                return halObj
        }
```

```
        modelDef.schema.post('save', function(doc, next) {
                db.model('Book').update({_id: doc.book}, {$addToSet: {reviews: this.
                id}}, function(err) {
                        next(err)
                })
        })
        return mongoose.model(modelDef.name, modelDef.schema)
}
```

/models/employee.js

```
var mongoose = require("mongoose"),
        jsonSelect = require('mongoose-json-select'),
        helpers = require("../lib/helpers"),
        _ = require("underscore")
module.exports = function(db) {
        var schema = require("../schemas/employee.js")
        var modelDef = db.getModelFromSchema(schema)
        modelDef.schema.methods.toHAL = function() {
                var halObj = helpers.makeHAL(this.toJSON())
                return halObj
        }
        return mongoose.model(modelDef.name, modelDef.schema)
}
```

/models/store.js

```
var mongoose = require("mongoose"),
        jsonSelect = require("mongoose-json-select"),
        _ = require("underscore"),
        helpers = require("../lib/helpers")
module.exports = function(db) {
        var schema = require("../schemas/store.js")
        var modelDef = db.getModelFromSchema(schema)
        modelDef.schema.plugin(jsonSelect, '-employees')
        modelDef.schema.methods.toHAL = function() {
                var halObj = helpers.makeHAL(this.toJSON(),
                                [{name: 'books', href: '/stores/' + this.id + '/
                                books', title: 'Books'},
                                {name: 'booksales', href: '/stores/' + this.id + '/
                                booksales', title: 'Book Sales'}])
                if(this.employees.length > 0) {
                        if(this.employees[0].toString().length != 24) {
                                halObj.addEmbed('employees', _.map(this.employees,
                                function(e) { return e.toHAL() }))
                        }
                }
```

```
                return halObj
        }

        var model = mongoose.model(modelDef.name, modelDef.schema)

        return model
}
```

request_schemas

This folder contains the JSON Schemas that will be used to validate the requests. They need to describe an object and its properties. We should be able to validate against the request object attribute that contains the parameters (normally `request.params`, but potentially something else, such as `request.body`).

Due to the type of attributes we defined for our endpoints, there is really only one endpoint that we would want to validate: the `getBookSales` (GET `/booksales`) endpoint. It receives two date parameters, and we probably want to validate their format to be 100% certain that the dates are valid.

Again, to provide the simplicity of usage that "convention over configuration" provides, our schema files must follow a very specific format, which is then used by the validator that we saw earlier:

```
/request_schemas/[CONTROLLER NAME].js
module.exports = {
 [ENDPOINT NICKNAME]: {
   validate: [TYPE],
   schema: [JSON SCHEMA]
 }
}
```

There are several pieces that need to be explained in the preceding code:

- CONTROLLER NAME: This means that the file for the schema needs to have the same name as the controller, all lowercase. And since we already did that for our controllers' files, this mean the schemas for each controller will have to have the same name as each controller's file.
- ENDPOINT NICKNAME: This should be the nickname given to the action when adding it to the controller (using the `addAction` method).
- TYPE: The type of object to validate. The only value supported right now is `params`, which references the query and path parameters received. This could be extended to support other objects.
- JSON SCHEMA: This is where we add the actual JSON Schema defining the request parameters.

Here is the actual code defining the validation for the `getBookSales` action.

/request_schemas/booksales.js

```
module.exports = {

 getbooksales: {
   validate: 'params',
   schema: {
     type: "object",
```

```
      properties: {
        start_date: {
          type: 'string',
          format:'date'
        },
        end_date: {
          type: 'string',
          format:'date'
        },
        store_id: {
          type: 'string'
        }
      }
    }
  }
}
```

schemas

This folder contains the JSON Schema definitions of our resources, which also translate into the Mongoose Schemas when initializing our models.

The level of detail provided in these files is very important, because it also translates into the actual Mongoose model. This means that we could define things such as ranges of values and format patterns, which would be validated by Mongoose when creating the new resources.

For instance, let's take a look at ClientReview, a schema that makes use of such capability.

/schemas/clientreview.js

```
module.exports = {
        "id": "ClicntReview",
        "properties": {
                "client": {
                        "$ref": "Client",
                        "description": "The client who submits the review"
                },
                "book": {
                        "$ref": "Book",
                        "description": "The book being reviewed"
                },
                "review_text": {
                        "type": "string",
                        "description": "The actual review text"
                },
                "stars": {
                        "type": "integer",
                        "description": "The number of stars, from 0 to 5",
                        "min": 0,
                        "max": 5
                }
        }
}
```

The stars attribute is clearly setting the maximum and minimum values that we can send when saving a new review. If we tried to send an invalid number, then we would get an error like the one shown in Figure 7-2.

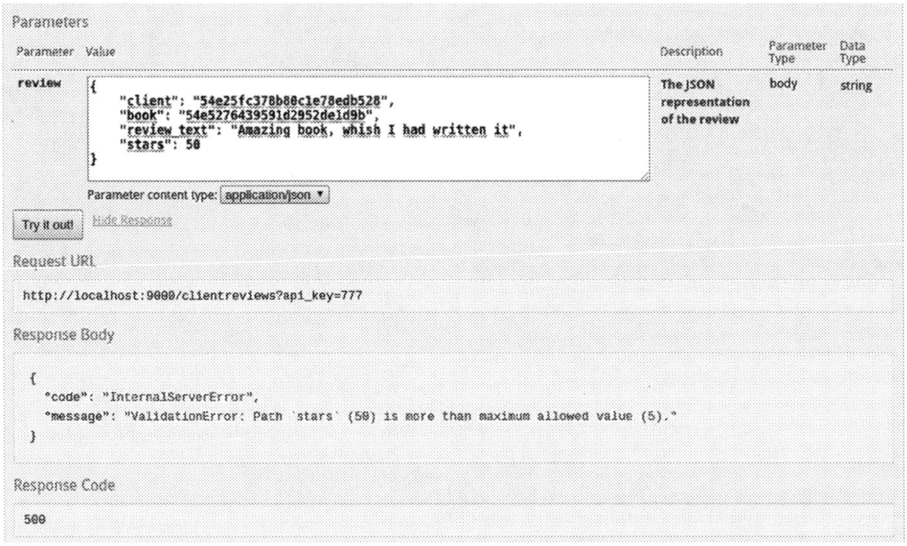

Figure 7-2. An error when trying to save an invalid value in a validated model

When defining schemas that reference others, remember to correctly name the reference (the name of each schema is given by the id property). So if you correctly set up the reference, the getModelFromSchema method of the db module will also properly set up the reference in Mongoose (this works both for direct reference and for collections).

Here is the main file for this folder; the index.js works like the index files in the other folders:

```
module.exports = {
        models: {
                BookSale: require("./booksale"),
                Book: require("./book"),
                Author: require("./author"),
                Store: require("./store"),
                Employee: require("./employee"),
                Client: require("./client"),
                ClientReview: require("./clientreview")
        }
}
```

Finally, here are the rest of the schemas defined for the project.

/schemas/author.js

```
module.exports = {
        "id": "Author",
        "properties": {
                "name": {
                        "type": "string",
                        "description": "The full name of the author"
                },
                "description": {
                        "type": "string",
                        "description": "A small bio of the author"
                },
                "books": {
                        "type": "array",
                        "description": "The list of books published on at least one
                        of the stores by this author",
                        "items": {
                                "$ref": "Book"
                        }
                },
                "website": {
                        "type": "string",
                        "description": "The Website url of the author"
                },
                "avatar": {
                        "type": "string",
                        "description": "The url for the avatar of this author"
                }
        }
}
```

/schemas/book.js

```
module.exports = {
        "id": "Book",
        "properties": {
                "title": {
                        "type": "string",
                        "description": "The title of the book"
                },
                "authors": {
                        "type":"array",
                        "description":"List of authors of the book",
                        "items": {
                                "$ref": "Author"
                        }
                },
```

```
                "isbn_code": {
                        "description": "Unique identifier code of the book",
                        "type":"string"
                },
                "stores": {
                        "type": "array",
                        "description": "The stores where clients can buy this book",
                        "items": {
                                "type": "object",
                                "properties": {
                                        "store": {
                                                "$ref": "Store",
                                        },
                                        "copies": {
                                                "type": "integer"
                                        }
                                }
                        }
                },
                "genre": {
                        "type": "string",
                        "description": "Genre of the book"
                },
                "description": {
                        "type": "string",
                        "description": "Description of the book"
                },
                "reviews": {
                        "type": "array",
                        "items": {
                                "$ref": "ClientReview"
                        }
                },
                "price": {
                        "type": "number",
                        "minimun": 0,
                        "description": "The price of this book"
                }
        }
}
```

/schemas/booksale.js

```
module.exports = {
        "id": "BookSale",
        "properties": {
                "date": {
                        "type":"date",
                        "description": "Date of the transaction"
                },
```

```
                "books": {
                        "type": "array",
                        "description": "Books sold",
                        "items": {
                                "$ref": "Book"
                        }
                },
                "store": {
                        "type": "object",
                        "description": "The store where this sale took place",
                        "type": "object",
                        "$ref": "Store"
                },
                "employee": {
                        "type": "object",
                        "description": "The employee who makes the sale",
                        "$ref": "Employee"
                },
                "client": {
                        "type": "object",
                        "description": "The person who gets the books",
                        "$ref": "Client",
                },
                "totalAmount": {
                        "type": "integer"
                }
        }
}
```

/schemas/client.js

```
module.exports = {
        "id": "Client",
        "properties": {
                "name": {
                        "type": "string",
                        "description": "Full name of the client"
                },
                "address": {
                        "type": "string",
                        "description": "Address of residence of this client"
                },
                "phone_number": {
                        "type": "string",
                        "description": "Contact phone number for the client"
                },
                "email": {
                        "type": "string",
                        "description": "Email of the client"
                }
        }
}
```

/schemas/employee.js

```
module.exports = {
        "id": "Employee",
        "properties": {
                "first_name": {
                        "type": "string",
                        "description": "First name of the employee"
                },
                "last_name": {
                        "type": "string",
                        "description": "Last name of the employee"
                },
                "birthdate": {
                        "type": "string",
                        "description": "Date of birth of this employee"
                },
                "address": {
                        "type": "string",
                        "description": "Address for the employee"
                },
                "phone_numbers": {
                        "type": "array",
                        "description": "List of phone numbers of this employee",
                        "items": {
                                "type": "string"
                        }
                },
                "email": {
                        "type": "string",
                        "description": "Employee's email"
                },
                "hire_date": {
                        "type": "string",
                        "description": "Date when this employee was hired"
                },
                "employee_number": {
                        "type": "number",
                        "description": "Unique identifier of the employee"
                }
        }
}
```

/schemas/store.js

```
module.exports = {
        "id": "Store",
        "properties": {
                "name": {
                        "type": "string",
                        "description": "The actual name of the store"
                },
```

```
                "address": {
                        "type": "string",
                        "description": "The address of the store"
                },
                "state": {
                        "type": "string",
                        "description": "The state where the store resides"
                },
                "phone_numbers": {
                        "type": "array",
                        "description": "List of phone numbers for the store",
                        "items": {
                                "type": "string"
                        }
                },
                "employees": {
                        "type": "array",
                        "description": "List of employees of the store",
                        "items": {
                                "$ref": "Employee"
                        }
                }
        }
}
```

swagger-ui

This folder contains the downloaded Swagger UI project, so we will not go over this particular code; however, I will mention the minor modifications we'll need to do to the `index.html` file (located at the root of the `swagger-ui` folder) to get the UI to properly load.

The changes needed are three very simple ones:

1. Edit the routes for all the resources loaded (CSS and JS files) to start with `swagger-ui/`.
2. Change the URL for the documentation server to `http://localhost:9000/api-docs` (around line 31).
3. Uncomment the block of code in line 73. Set the right value to the `apiKey` variable (set it to 777).

With those changes, the UI should be able to load correctly and allow you to start testing your API.

Root Folder

This is the root of the project. There are only two files here: the main `index.js` and the `package.json` file that contains the dependencies and other project attributes.

/package.json

```
{
  "name": "come_n_read",
  "version": "1.0.0",
  "description": "",
  "main": "index.js",
  "scripts": {
    "test": "echo \"Error: no test specified\" && exit 1"
  },
  "author": "",
  "license": "ISC",
  "dependencies": {
    "colors": "^1.0.3",
    "halson": "^2.3.1",
    "mongoose": "^3.8.23",
    "mongoose-json-select": "^0.2.1",
    "restify": "^2.8.5",
    "swagger-node-restify": "^0.1.2",
    "tv4": "^1.1.9",
    "tv4-formats": "^1.0.0",
    "underscore": "^1.7.0"
  }
}
```

The most interesting part of this file is the list of dependencies. The rest was autogenerated using the `init` option of the `npm` command-line tool.

/index.js

```
var restify = require("restify"),
        colors = require("colors"),
        lib = require("./lib"),
        swagger = require("swagger-node-restify"),
        config = lib.config

var server = restify.createServer(lib.config.server)

//Middleware setup
server.use(restify.queryParser())
server.use(restify.bodyParser())

restify.defaultResponseHeaders = function(data) {
  this.header('Access-Control-Allow-Origin', '*')
}

///Middleware to check for valid api key sent
server.use(function(req, res, next) {
        //We move forward if we're dealing with the swagger-ui or a valid key
        if(req.url.indexOf("swagger-ui") != -1 || lib.helpers.validateKey(req.
        headers.hmacdata || '', req.params.api_key, lib)) {
                next()
        } else {
```

```
                res.send(401, { error: true, msg: 'Invalid api key sent'})
        }
})
/**
Validate each request, as long as there is a schema for it
*/
server.use(function(req, res, next) {
        var results = lib.schemaValidator.validateRequest(req)
        if(results.valid) {
                next()
        } else {
                res.send(400, results)
        }
})
//the swagger-ui is inside the "swagger-ui" folder
server.get(/^\/swagger-ui(\/.*)?/, restify.serveStatic({
        directory: __dirname + '/',
        default: 'index.html'
 }))
//setup section
swagger.addModels(lib.schemas)
swagger.setAppHandler(server)
lib.helpers.setupRoutes(server, swagger, lib)
swagger.configureSwaggerPaths("", "/api-docs", "") //we remove the {format} part of
the paths, to
swagger.configure('http://localhost:9000', '0.1')
//start the server
server.listen(config.server.port, function() {
        console.log("Server started succesfully…".green)
        lib.db.connect(function(err) {
                if(err) console.log("Error trying to connect to database: ".red,
                err.red)
                else console.log("Database service successfully started".green)
        })
})
```

And finally, the main file, the one that starts it all up, the `index.js`. There are four distinct sections to this file:

- The *initial section,* which requires all needed modules and instantiates the server.
- The *middleware setup section,* which handles setting up all pieces of middleware (we'll go over this in a bit).
- The *setup section,* which handles loading models, controllers, setting up routes, and whatnot.
- The *server start section,* which starts the web server and the database client.

The initial and final sections of the file don't really require much explanation since they're pretty self-explanatory, so let's go over the other two.

Middleware Setup

The middleware setup is potentially the most important part of the file and of the bootstrap process required for the API to start up and function properly. But thanks to the ease of use and simplicity that the middleware mechanics bring to the table, it's very easy to write and understand.

We're setting up five different middleware here:

- The *query parser* to turn the query parameters into an object so that we can access them easily.
- The *body parser* so that we can access the content of the POST and PUT requests as an object, with the added bonus of autoparsing JSON strings.
- The *security check*, which takes care of rehashing the request every time to make sure that we're dealing with an authenticated client.
- The *validate check*, which validates the request against any existing JSON Schema.
- The *static content folder*, which is not exactly a middleware, but acts as one for one specific set of routes, allowing Restify to serve static content.

Setup Section

This last section is also very important; those five lines actually handles instantiating all the models, linking Swagger and the Restify server, setting up all the routes (linking the code of each action to the corresponding path and method defined in the spec section), and finally, setting up the route for the Swagger back-end server.

Summary

Congratulations! You should now have a working version of our API, capable of doing pretty much everything we set up to do in Chapter 6. You should also have a better understanding of how these modules work. Ideally, you'll consider them for your next project. Of course, there are alternatives like the ones discussed in Chapter 5, so don't forget about those either.

In the final chapter of the book, I'll go over some of the most common issues you might encounter when dealing with this type of project, and you'll see how to solve them.

CHAPTER 8

Troubleshooting

This is it. You made it to the final chapter. You experienced firsthand what it takes to write a RESTful API in Node. You've gone over the theory. You learned what REST actually stands for and how to use it to develop a good and useful API.

In this chapter, I'll cover some of the things that can go wrong during the process and some of the considerations you have to take into account, such as the following:

- Asynchronous programming. I'll take one final shot at this subject, explaining how it was used in our code.
- Minor details about the Swagger UI configuration. Sometimes the documentation is not enough.
- Potential CORS issues. I'll go over the basics of CORS to help you understand how to use it to your advantage.
- Data types. The last subject that I'll cover regarding our code is how to go from JSON Schemas data types to Mongoose types.

Asynchronous Programming

For the mind of the non-JavaScript developer, or even for the non-Node.js developer, the concept of asynchronous programming might be a strange one to grasp at first. And I say "might" because it's not a JavaScript/Node.js-unique concept; other programming languages, like Earlang, Python, and even the more recent Go have this capacity.

That being said, Node.js is one of the few environments where a web developer is kind of forced to deal with this concept or is unable to properly develop.

Asynchronous programming becomes a must on any mid-sized project using Node.js when you start dealing with external resources, mainly because that means you'll be using third-party libraries that are already taking advantage of this programming technique; so you either embrace it or switch languages.

You've already covered how this feature improves the performance of applications, and you even saw a couple of useful design patterns that leverage it, so let's now discuss how failing to grasp this concept could hurt your understanding of the code presented in Chapter 7.

Whether or not you've noticed, in our API's code, there are several places where asynchronous programming takes place. Let's look at some of them.

F. Doglio, *Pro REST API Development with Node.js*, DOI 10.1007/978-1-4842-0917-2_8

The Controllers Action's Code

Every action on every controller has a piece of asynchronous programming in the form of database queries. This is probably the most obvious bit, but it's important to go over it to understand it properly.

The reason why we don't do anything like this:

```
var authors = lib.db.model('Author')
   .find(criteria).exec()

if(!authors) return next(controller.RESTError('InternalServerError', authors))
controller.writeHAL(res, authors)
```

And instead, we set up a callback function, like this:

```
lib.db.model('Author')
   .find(criteria)
   .exec(function(err, authors) {
       if(err) return next(controller.RESTError('InternalServerError', err))
       controller.writeHAL(res, authors)
   })
```

This is because, as I've already stated, I/O operations in Node.js are *asynchronous*, which means that querying the database needs to be done like this, with a callback function set up to handle the response once it arrives. It is true that Node.js provides synchronous versions of its I/O functions (like reading and writing files) but they're mostly there to simplify the transition; you're not being encouraged to use them, and third-party libraries like Mongoose aren't interested in following that pattern either.

Catching this type of error while manually testing your application might be a bit of a headache, because the resulting behavior might not always be the same. When the code is complex enough, it becomes a race between the time it takes for the asynchronous function to get a response back and the time it takes for your code to use that value.

Also, because the Node.js interpreter won't throw an error if you miss some of the parameters on a method/function call, you might end up doing something like this:

```
function libraryMethod(attr1, callback) {
 asyncCall(attr1, function(response){
     if(callback) callback(response)
 })
}
var returnValue = libraryMethod('hello world')
```

The preceding code will not throw an error—ever. And you'll always get undefined in your `returnValue`. And if you don't have access to the code of the `libraryMethod` function, it might be difficult to understand what's wrong. For instance, you have a code like this:

```
var myResponseValue = ''
asyncCall('hello', function(response) {
   myResponseValue = response
})
///some other code taking 30ms to execute
console.log(myResponseValue)
```

The preceding code shows another common mistake when working with asynchronous calls: you properly set up the callback, but you used the returned value outside of that callback.

In the preceding example, if the asyncCall takes less than 30 milliseconds to get a response, it'll work but you won't realize your mistake until something happens (such as the code going to production). Suddenly, asyncCall takes 31 milliseconds to execute, and now "undefined" is always printing to the console. But you don't know why, of course. The simple way to fix this is to add any code dealing with the response value *inside* the callback function.

The Middleware Functions

This might not be obvious at first glance, but the entire middleware chain is following the serial flow mechanics mentioned back in Chapter 3. How can you tell? Because of the next function; you need to call it when the function is over and ready to give control to the next middleware.

You can have even more asynchronous code inside the function and still be able to call the next function, thanks to next. In some places this isn't really visible, like when setting up the queryParser and bodyParser middleware:

```
server.use(restify.queryParser())
server.use(restify.bodyParser())
```

But those methods are actually returning a new function, which in turn receives the three magic parameters: the request object, the response object, and the next function.

A common issue when creating custom middleware is forgetting to call the next function in one of the possible execution branches of your code (if you happen to have them). Symptoms of this are that your API appears to hang up, you never get a response back from the server, and you don't see any errors on the console. This is due to the fact that the execution flow is broken. Suddenly it's unable to find a way to continue. And you're not sending back a response (using the response object). This is a tricky to catch, since there aren't any error messages to clearly state the problem.

```
function middleware(req, res, next){
  if(req.params.q == '1') {
      next()
  } else {
     if(req.params.q2 == '1') {
        next()
     }
  }
  //if no 'q' or 'q2' parameters are sent, or if they don't have the right values, then this
middleware is breaking the serial flow and no response is ever getting back to the client.
}
```

There is another type of middleware used on the project: Mongoose middleware, which are the hooks you can attach to models to be executed before or after a set of specific actions. Our particular case used a post save hook on the clientreview model:

```
modelDef.schema.post('save', function(doc, next) {
        db.model('Book').update({_id: doc.book}, {$addToSet: {reviews: this.id}},
function(err) {
     next(err)
        })
   })
```

This code clearly shows the `next` function being used in conjunction with an asynchronous call inside the middleware. If you were to forget to call `next`, then the execution would be interrupted (and halted) at this callback.

Issues Configuring the Swagger UI

Setting up the Swagger UI is a task that requires both a change to the UI itself and some special code on the back end. This is not particularly easy to understand since the documentation is not exactly simple to read.

On the one hand, we're using the swagger-node-restify module to generate the back-end endpoints needed by the UI; this is achieved in the following lines:

1. `swagger.addModels(lib.schemas)`
2. `swagger.setAppHandler(server)`
3. `lib.helpers.setupRoutes(server, swagger, lib)`
4. `swagger.configureSwaggerPaths("", "/api-docs", "")`
5. `swagger.configure('http://localhost:9000', '0.1')`

Line 1 sets up the models, so that Swagger can return them when the endpoints specify them as the response class. Line 2 is basically telling the module which web server we are using for the documentation. We could potentially have two different servers configured: one for the documentation and one for the actual API.

Line 3 is actually one of ours, but it does require Swagger, because we're calling the `addGET`, `addPOST`, `addDELETE`, or `addPUT` methods provided by it (this is done by the `BaseController` code in its `setUpActions` method).

Line 4 doesn't really say much, but it's useful for several reasons:

- The most obvious one is that we're setting up the path for the documentation: `/api-docs`.
- We're also saying that we don't want to specify formats via extension (i.e., `.json`). By default, we need to define a {format} section in our path to be autoreplaced by `.json`. With this specific line, we're removing the need for that and simplifying the path formats.

Finally, line 5 sets the base URL for the entire documentation API.

In Chapter 7, the front-end code had to change; I mentioned where exactly. Uncommenting the code for the API key and the change in the host URL are obviously needed, but the change in the resource path isn't. We need to change this because of the way we configured the static path during the initialization phase.

```
server.get(/^\/swagger-ui(\/.*)?/, restify.serveStatic({
        directory: __dirname + '/',
        default: 'index.html'
}))
```

The preceding code is making sure that only anything under the `swagger-ui` folder is served as static content (which is basically everything that the Swagger UI needs), but the default path that comes in the HTML file points to the root folder, which isn't good enough in our case.

CORS: a.k.a. Cross-Origin Resource Sharing

Any web developer who's been at it for a while has seen this dreaded error message:

```
XMLHttpRequest cannot load http://domain.example. Origin http://domain1.example is not
allowed by Access-Control-Allow-Origin.
```

For developers working on a web client for a public API, the browser checks for *cross-origin resource sharing* (CORS) to make sure that the request is secure, which means that the browser checked the requested endpoint and since it's not finding any CORS headers, or the headers don't specify our domain as valid, it is cancelling the request for security reasons.

For API designers, this is a very relevant error because CORS needs to be taken into account, either by manually allowing it or by denying it. If you're designing a public API, you need to make sure that you specify in the response headers that any domain can make a request. This is the most permissive of all possible settings. If, on the other hand, you're defining a private API, then the CORS headers help define the only domains that can actually request any kind of resource of the endpoints.

Normally, a web client will follow a set of steps on every CORS request:

1. First, the client will ask the API server if the desired request is possible (Can the client query the wanted resource using the needed method from the current origin?). This is done by sending a "pre-flight"[1] request with the `Access-Control-Request-Header` header (with the headers the client needs to access) and the `Access-Control-Request-Method` header (with the method needed).

2. Then the server will answer with what is authorized, using these headers: `Access-Control-Allow-Origin` with the allowed origin (or * for anything), `Access-Control-Allowed-Methods` with the valid methods, and `Access-Control-Allow-Headers` with a list of valid headers to be sent.

3. Finally, the client can do the "normal" request.

If anything fails to validate during the pre-flight request (either the requested method or the headers needed), then the response will not be a 200 OK response.

For our case, according to the code in Chapter 7, we're going for the public API approach, since we're allowing any domains to do requests to our endpoints with the following code:

```
restify.defaultResponseHeaders = function(data) {
 this.header('Access-Control-Allow-Origin', '*')
}
```

Data Types

Even though we're not directly handling and specifying types for our variables throughout the API's JavaScript code, there are two very specific places where data types are needed: the JSON Schemas defined for our resources and the Mongoose models defined.

Now, thanks to the code in the `getModelFromSchema` function and the `translateTypeToJs` function, you can go from JSON Schema types to Mongoose types because most of the basic types defined in our schemas, are almost directly translatable into JavaScript types.

For the more complex types, like arrays, since the entire definition is different, extra code needs to be added, which is where the `getModelFromSchema` code comes in.

---

[1]An OPTIONS request.

The type's translation from the code in Chapter 7 is limited to what was needed at the time, but you could easily extend it to achieve further functionalities, like getting the `required` attribute to work for both the schema validator and the Mongoose validators (these make sure you don't save anything invalid). Let's quickly look at how to go about adding support for the `required` property.

An *object* type is composed of a series of properties, but also, a list of required properties, which is defined at the same level as the `properties` attribute:

```
module.exports = {
    "id": "Author",
    "properties": {
        "name": {
           "type": "string",
           "description": "The full name of the author"
        },
        "description": {
           "type": "string",
           "description": "A small bio of the author"
        },
        "books": {
           "type": "array",
           "description": "The list of books published on at least one of the stores by this
           author",
           "items": {
              "$ref": "Book"
           }
        },
        "website": {
           "type": "string",
           "description": "The Website url of the author"
        },
        "avatar": {
           "type": "string",
           "description": "The url for the avatar of this author"
        },
        "address": {
           "type": "object",
           "properties": {
              "street": {
                 "type": "string"
           },
              "house_number": {
                 "type": "integer"
              }
           }
        }
    },
 "required": ["name", "website"]
}
```

To get the content of this new property, you just need to add a few lines to the getModelFromSchema function to simply check for the property name; and if it's inside the required array, you set it as required:

```
function getModelFromSchema(schema) {
    var data = {
        name: schema.id,
        schema: {}
    }

    var newSchema = {}
    var tmp = null
    var requiredProperties = schema.required

    _.each(schema.properties, function(v, propName) {
if( requiredProperties && requiredProperties.indexOf(propName) != -1) {
v.required = true
        }
        if(v['$ref'] != null) {
tmp = {
    type: Schema.ObjectId,
    ref: v['$ref']
}
        } else {
tmp = translateComplexType(v)
        }
        newSchema[propName] = tmp
    })
    data.schema = new Schema(newSchema)
    return data
```

Summary

This is it. You made it. And you managed to go through the entire book! You went from the basics of REST to a full-blown RESTful API, and finally, in this chapter, you learned the main things that can cause trouble during the development process, such as asynchronous programming, configuring the Swagger UI, CORS, and moving from JSON Schema types to Mongoose types.

Thank you for reading and, hopefully, enjoying the book.

Index

F. Doglio, *Pro REST API Development with Node.js*, DOI 10.1007/978-1-4842-0917-2

G

H

I

J, K

L

M

N

O

P

Q

R

S

T, U

V

W

X, Y, Z